ORTHO'S All A...

Basements,
Attics, and Bonus Rooms'

Meredith® Books
Des Moines, Iowa

Ortho® Books
An imprint of Meredith® Books
All About Basements, Attics, and Bonus Rooms
Editor: Larry Johnston
Contributing Writer: Martin Miller
Senior Associate Design Director: Tom Wegner
Assistant Editor: Harijs Priekulis
Copy Chief: Terri Fredrickson
Managers, Book Production: Pam Kvitne,
    Marjorie J. Schenkelberg
Contributing Copy Editor: Steve Hallam
Technical Proofreader: Ray Kast
Contributing Proofreaders: Beth Lastine, Debra Morris
    Smith, Tricia Toney
Indexer: Barbara L. Klein
Electronic Production Coordinator: Paula Forest
Editorial and Design Assistants: Kathleen Stevens,
    Karen Schirm

Additional Editorial Contributions from
    Art Rep Services
Director: Chip Nadeau
Designer: lk Design
Illustrator: Dave Brandon

Meredith® Books
Editor in Chief: James D. Blume
Design Director: Matt Strelecki
Managing Editor: Gregory H. Kayko
Executive Editor, Gardening and Home Improvement:
    Benjamin W. Allen
Executive Editor, Home Improvement: Larry Erickson

Director, Sales, Special Markets: Rita McMullen
Director, Sales, Premiums: Michael A. Peterson
Director, Sales, Retail: Tom Wierzbicki
Director, Book Marketing: Brad Elmitt
Director, Operations: George A. Susral
Director, Production: Douglas M. Johnston

Meredith Publishing Group
President, Publishing Group: Stephen M. Lacy

Meredith Corporation
Chairman and Chief Executive Officer: William T. Kerr

Chairman of the Executive Committee: E.T. Meredith III

Photographers
(Photographers credited may retain copyright ©
to the listed photographs.)
L = Left, R = Right, C = Center, B = Bottom, T = Top
King Au/Studio Au, 4BL
Laurie Black, 6CL
Ross Chapple, 12B
Mike Dieter, 64, 76
D. Randolph Foulds, 7TR
Bob Hawks, 6TL
Bill Holt, 4BR
Thomas Hooper, 11CR
Inside Out Studios, 12T, 31T, 31B, 71TR
Wm. Hopkins, 11T
Beth Singer, 9TR
William Stites, 5T, 5CR
Rick Taylor, 8TL

All of us at Ortho® Books are dedicated to providing you
with the information and ideas you need to enhance your
home and garden. We welcome your comments and
suggestions about this book. Write to us at:
    Meredith Corporation
    Ortho Books
    1716 Locust St.
    Des Moines, IA 50309–3023

If you would like to purchase any of our home improvement,
gardening, cooking, crafts, or home decorating and design
books, check wherever quality books are sold. Or visit us at:
meredithbooks.com

If you would like more information on other Ortho
products, call 800-225-2883 or visit us at: www.ortho.com

ROOMS TO GROW 4

A Gallery of Design Ideas 6
The Finishing Touches 12

MAKING YOUR IDEA WORK 14

Changing the Space 16
Improving Access and Storage 18
Altering the Systems 20
Letting the Light In 22
Keeping the Moisture Out 23

MAKING PLANS 24

Build Within Your Budget 25
Drawing Plans 26
Do It Yourself or Hire a Pro? 28

CONSTRUCTION BASICS 30

Floor Basics 32
Wall Basics 36
Door and Window Basics 40
Stair Basics 44
Wiring Basics 46
Plumbing Basics 48

REMODELING YOUR ATTIC 50

Installing Attic Stairs 51
New Attic Floors and Ceilings 52
Building a Shed Dormer 54
Building a Gable Dormer 56
Building Attic Walls 58
Installing Attic Windows and Doors 60
Skylights and Roof Windows 62
Installing Vents and Insulation 63

REMODELING YOUR BASEMENT 64

Keeping Things Dry 65
Building Basement Stairs 66
Preparing a Basement Floor 68
Building Basement Walls 70
Installing Basement Doors and Windows 72

FINISHING TOUCHES 76

Installing Parquet or Vinyl Tile 78
Installing a Floating Floor 80
Installing Sheet Vinyl 82
Installing Conventional Carpet 84
Installing Drywall 86
Installing Wood Paneling 88
Finishing the Ceiling 90
Closets, Cabinets, and Shelving 92
Trim Work 94

4

IN THIS SECTION

A Gallery of
Design Ideas **6**
The Finishing
Touches **12**

ROOMS TO GROW

Creating new living space within your home is a rewarding adventure. Whether you need more room to accommodate a growing family, to entertain, or to set up a home office, your attic, basement, or bonus room offers space.

Putting vacant space to use requires decisions about function, style, materials, construction, and furnishings.

Planning is a key element in the project. That's the purpose of this book. You'll find information about every step your remodeling will require, starting with design schemes.

You'll also find solutions to problems that may be standing in the way of your dream room and tips that will make your plans go more smoothly. You will need to decide whether to do the work yourself or hire a contractor for all or part of it. This book shows what's involved in the many aspects of the job so you can make the right decisions.

Step-by-step instructions show various construction techniques such as wall building, window and door installation, and electrical and plumbing basics. Illustrations show you how to use these techniques in an attic, basement, or bonus room conversion.

No matter how ambitious your goals, this book has the information you need to make the journey go smoothly from start to finish.

Transform unused attic space into a comfortable master suite. Skylights and gable-end windows bring light into this inviting room.

Attics are full of architectural novelty. Roof angles and framing often create cozy, inviting spaces. The roof design adds interest to this bedroom sitting area.

It takes some work, but you can bring natural light into a basement. Here the basement wall has been bumped out into a dugout with insulated greenhouse windows to brighten a multipurpose room.

MAKE A WISH

To simplify your planning and maintain family harmony, gather the family and:
■ Make a wish list of things each family member wants in the home. Use your imagination, but keep descriptions simple. Then prioritize the list.
■ Make a needs list and match it with the family wish list. Make decisions about what you need and what you can do without. This brainstorming will provide a foundation for your planning.

Outside the room, plantings and a brick walk integrate the bumped-out basement solarium into the landscape. An exterior entrance ties the room to the backyard.

DISCOVERING YOUR STYLE

Here are some steps that will help you find your style:
■ Read decorating magazines and home decorating books. Cut or copy photos of rooms, furniture, and accessories that appeal to you. Put your clippings in a folder.
■ When you visit friends' homes, make mental notes of room arrangements, colors, and other decorative aspects. Notice things you like and don't like. Ask them about the advantages and disadvantages of floor or wallcoverings. Jot down your impressions when you get home and put your notes in the folder.
■ Visit home furnishing stores, decorating showrooms, and home improvement outlets. Collect material samples, brochures, and paint chips to put in your folder.
■ When you're ready to plan your room, review your collection of design ideas. Make notes about the colors, textures, and patterns that appeal to you, then narrow them down to those you think will look best in your new room.
■ Design the space based on these preferences, the purpose of the room, and the furnishings you'll use.

BUILDING CODES

Building codes are enacted by almost all communities to ensure construction methods and materials are consistent and safe. Throughout this book, you'll find sections that outline national code requirements for lighting, plumbing, and other aspects of construction. These sections are only guides; your local codes may have more restrictive requirements.

Once you have a rough plan in mind for your remodeling project, visit your local building department to find out what codes apply to your work, what permits you will need, and what inspections will be required during the work.

A GALLERY OF DESIGN IDEAS

A basement often allows room for space-consuming items like this billiard table. Dark-stained and -painted structural elements give more visual headroom than a ceiling would.

This cozy office/den combination tucks into a bonus area between the house and garage. It also includes a mudroom and entry.

In the early stages of planning an additional room, base all aspects of a room's design on how you intend to use it.

For example, if you want a bedroom and an office in separate rooms, each should incorporate design elements specific to its use. But combining a bedroom and office in the same space changes the requirements. You'll need a larger room with a decorative scheme that unifies the space and keeps the two functions separate and distinct.

Clarify your goals before you start building walls. A well-thought-out plan will save time and money and give you added living space you will enjoy long after the dust of remodeling has settled.

FAMILY ROOMS

Attics, basements, and bonus rooms make perfect family rooms because they're removed from traffic patterns and daily activities, they usually contain plenty of space, and you can change them as the family grows.

Be sure to plan for the future: Family rooms, like families, change. The family room of 20 years ago may not have included much more than comfortable seating and a TV set. The family room of today serves a number of roles—a place not just to watch TV, but to use a whole wall of media modules, to carry out hobby or office activity, and even to use recreational equipment.

Here are some tips that will make your family room practical, comfortable, and enjoyable:

■ Make the atmosphere cheery—decorate it with brightly colored furniture and accents that reflect your personality.

■ Open the room to light with a south-facing window or skylight, but protect it from direct sunlight or glare with window coverings.

■ Arrange seating so it's comfortable—make conversation groupings at least 10 feet square, with no more than 8 feet between any two people. For TV viewing, place seats no farther than 10 to 12 feet from the screen and at no more than a 45-degree angle from it.

■ Add tables and countertops for games, hobbies, and snacking.

■ Install a kitchenette for casual food preparation—an apartment-sized sink, refrigerator, and counter will do the job.

■ Build in cabinetry that will attractively display—or hide—your media equipment. Mix open shelving with drawer units and storage protected by doors.

■ Plan electrical wiring for the future. Wire the room with enough outlets, and install special circuits for any equipment that needs them.

RECOMMENDED ROOM SIZES

Room	Minimum Area*	Minimum Size	Preferred Size
Bedroom	80 sq. ft.	8×10 ft.	11×14 ft.
Master bedroom	Not specified		12×16 ft.
Family room	110 sq. ft.	10½×10½ ft.	12×16 ft.
Living room	176 sq. ft.	11×16 ft.	12×18 ft.
Other habitable room	70 sq. ft.	7×10 ft.	
Bathroom	35 sq. ft.	5×7 ft.	5×9 ft.
Apartment	400 sq. ft.		

U.S. Department of Housing and Urban Development minimum net floor area within enclosed walls, excluding built-in fixtures, closets, and cabinets.

OFFICES

Whether you need a professional office or simply want a place to take care of household business, your home office space should be set apart from household traffic. The ideal office should offer convenient access, privacy, quiet, sufficient record storage, and enough room to conduct your business affairs comfortably.

Plan your office so that your working surfaces are at least 29 inches deep and 30 inches from the floor. Allow enough space for file cabinets, computer equipment, and desk accessories, but if you have additional space, go ahead and use it. You may need only an area for computing taxes and paying bills now, but those needs may change. If you will be conducting business from the office, include these elements in your plans:

■ Make a creative office atmosphere conducive to work and client meetings. Windows and interior lighting should be functional as well as decorative.

■ Locate the office near an outside doorway or interior stairs so visitors and delivery persons can come and go easily.

■ Soundproof the basement stairwell and ceiling (or attic floor) to keep other family activities from interfering with work.

■ Multiple work surfaces will help you manage several projects at once. Arrange the work areas so you can convert them to conference space.

This office sits under a dormer above the garage. Custom-made windows on the side let in extra light.

MINIMUM CLEARANCES FOR FURNISHINGS

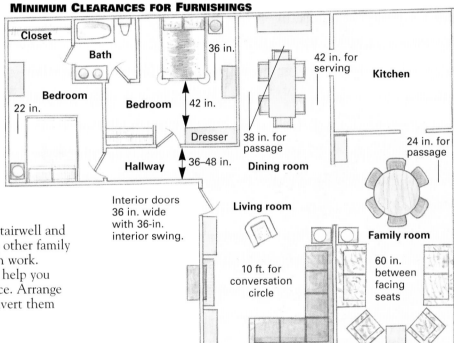

Closet

Bath

Bedroom

22 in.

Bedroom

Hallway

36 in.

42 in.

Dresser

36–48 in.

38 in. for passage

Dining room

42 in. for serving

Kitchen

24 in. for passage

Family room

60 in. between facing seats

Living room

10 ft. for conversation circle

Interior doors 36 in. wide with 36-in. interior swing.

MINIMUM HEADROOM REQUIREMENTS

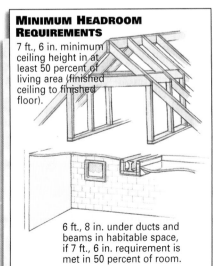

7 ft., 6 in. minimum ceiling height in at least 50 percent of living area (finished ceiling to finished floor).

6 ft., 8 in. under ducts and beams in habitable space, if 7 ft., 6 in. requirement is met in 50 percent of room.

BUILDING CODES FOR HABITABLE ROOMS

A habitable room is one used for sleeping, living, cooking, or eating. Closets, hallways, baths, laundries, and utility rooms are not habitable.

ROOM SIZE: Habitable rooms must have at least 70 square feet of floor area (50 square feet for kitchens) with one horizontal dimension of at least 7 feet.

CEILING HEIGHT: Habitable rooms must have ceiling heights of at least 7½ feet in 50 percent of their areas (7 feet in kitchens). No portion of the room may have a ceiling height of less than 5 feet. Beams and girders spaced at least 4 feet on center may hang a maximum of 6 inches below a finished ceiling.

EXITS: Sleeping rooms must have at least one exterior door or an egress window that can be opened. Egress windowsills must be no more than 44 inches above the finished floor. The window must have a minimum clear width of 20 inches, a minimum clear height of 22 inches, and a minimum clear opening of 5.7 square feet.

A GALLERY OF DESIGN IDEAS
continued

Attics often seem remote from the rest of the house, but that seclusion can be an asset to a bedroom. Bring in plenty of light—enlarge an existing window, or add skylights or new windows in a gable wall.

ADDING AN APARTMENT?

If you have at least 400 square feet of floor area, you might be able to add an apartment in your attic, basement, or bonus room. But your local building codes must allow it and the space must meet the rest of the codes for a habitable room.

Building codes vary from place to place and are often based on lot size, existing number of bedrooms, residential zoning and covenant restrictions, and other requirements related to safety and neighborhood concerns. Before planning an apartment, check with your local officials.

BEDROOMS

Your first consideration when picking a bedroom location is probably seclusion, but make sure the room is large enough to house the bed, dresser, other furnishings, and closet space. Use the recommendations in the chart on page 6 as a guide.

Make attic nooks and crannies part of your decorating scheme—whether romantic and old-fashioned or sleek and modern. Attics can heat up in the summer, so you may need to enlarge your cooling system or add windows.

Basements, on the other hand, generally stay cool even in hot climates. Using a little creativity, you can make a basement bedroom comfortable and attractive. Basements often provide easy access to plumbing lines, which makes a bed-and-bath suite feasible.

Wherever you locate the bedroom, make sure you include an egress door or window (see code requirements on page 7).

Here are some more tips that go hand-in-hand with bedroom planning:
■ Access to your bedroom will affect your comfort; change awkard stair configurations for convenient entry and exit.
■ Install hard-wired smoke alarms outside each bedroom door and at the top of the stairs. Include the alarms in your wiring plans.
■ Soundproof the attic floor (or basement ceiling) to keep family noise out of your private retreat.
■ Plan for comfort and convenience. Consider a full or half bath close to the bedroom (with a luxurious tub and two sinks for a master suite) or a laundry chute for an attic location. Add carpet on the floor of a basement bedroom and install a bedside telephone. Be sure to include plenty of ventilation (window area equal to one-tenth of the room area is standard) and maximum closet space.

DON'T OVERBUILD FOR YOUR NEIGHBORHOOD

When planning to remodel new space in your home, ask yourself, "How much money am I willing to commit to this project?" The answer to this question can depend on how long you plan to stay in your home.

If you know you will move sometime in the future, find out how much (if any) your renovation will increase your house's value. Some conversions have no effect.

By some estimates, adding a bathroom to your house can increase the value of the house by up to 90 percent of the cost of the remodeling project; a new home office, as much as 60 percent of its cost. The actual return depends on location, the quality of the work in the project, and local real estate market conditions. A real estate appraiser can give you local estimates.

Increasing the value of your home by more than 15 percent of the average price in your neighborhood will make it more difficult to sell. Check with a real estate agent to verify your estimates.

If you plan to stay in your home for years, your decision will rest more on the increased long-term comfort of your home than on its resale value.

ROOMS FOR CHILDREN

Planning children's rooms requires balancing the size of the space, access for supervision, and sound control—for both the noise the children make and outside sounds that can wake them.

If your children are young, you'll want convenient access so you can supervise them—a first-floor bonus room might be best. Basements can be ideal for older kids. The low ceilings, high windows, and posts that are often parts of basement construction are of little concern to youngsters. The solid floors and walls will take a lot of abuse, and it's easy to control basement noise.

No matter where you put the children's room, keep the following in mind:

■ Make sure the floor area—their playground—is spacious and uncluttered and that you can modify it as the children grow.

■ Use a space-saving bunk or trundle bed and add storage for books, games, and all of the other things kids collect (storage bins on casters make cleanup easy).

■ Build a table or child's work surface for drawing and painting.

Seclusion is the key to this bedroom location. Dressers built into the knee walls make great use of otherwise lost space and reduce crowding in this room.

A teenager's bedroom often doubles as a retreat. This upstairs bedroom gains floor space for activities by opening into a small attic to give room for a loft bed.

Capitalize on architectural oddities in an attic to create a playroom with separate activity centers. Add sleeping areas to make a children's suite. The carpeted floor in this play area reduces noise in the room and below.

A GALLERY OF DESIGN IDEAS
continued

Portions of the flooring have been removed from this attic to create a music room in a loft overlooking the living room. The new skylight lets light into the loft and living room. Stainless steel posts and cables from a boat supplier make up the railing.

HOBBY ROOMS

A hobby room can go almost anywhere, whether it's a studio for painting, a model-building center, a chamber for your chamber music, a sewing room, or meditation space. Attics, basements, and bonus rooms all offer the out-of-the-way location that most homeowners want in a hobby room. When planning a hobby room, be sure to include:
■ Easy-to-clean floors and work surfaces.
■ Counter space to spread out comfortably.
■ Well-placed ambient lighting and direct lighting over work areas.
■ A sink, if your hobby requires cleanup.
■ Sufficient ventilation from windows or a forced-air system to exhaust any fumes produced by glue or paint.
■ Lockable storage to protect materials and children.

HOME WORKSHOPS

This is the dream space of every do-it-yourselfer, and although you might first think of putting it in the

Hobby work can be as serious as office work, and requires plenty of space, as well as ample direct lighting. This sewing center includes storage and plenty of work surfaces.

garage, consider that you can heat your basement more easily than your garage. Here's what you need for a well-planned workshop:
■ Light-colored walls and bright, general lighting.
■ Locked storage for hazardous substances, an efficient ventilation system, and a fire extinguisher within close reach.
■ A centralized vacuum dust-collection system with outlets for each power tool.
■ Electrical outlets in the ceiling for stationary equipment and along the edge of workbenches for portable power tools.
■ Workbenches and rolling storage on lockable casters.
■ Soft, removable, area floor coverings—rubber or vinyl mats lift for easy cleaning.
■ Wall-mounted tool storage, as well as storage under workbenches.
■ Work zones—separate areas for benches, portable tools, and stationary tools.

WINE CELLARS

Once considered the province of the ultra-rich, wine cellars are now finding wider use in homes. Temperature control is a primary concern, as are insulated walls between the cellar and other heated spaces. Make sure your wine cellar plans include:
■ Window coverings to keep out direct sunlight.
■ A solid floor that won't vibrate.
■ Storage racks capable of holding different-sized bottles, as well as floor and shelf space for cases.

FITNESS/RECREATION CENTERS

At first, you may think a basement is the only space suitable for a fitness and recreation center. You can also include such areas in your attic or bonus room plans, however. With modern noise-suppression materials and hefty construction in attic floors or bonus room walls, you can create a place where family members can exercise without disturbing other family activities. In addition to sound insulation, you'll need:
■ A room measuring at least 12×16 feet.
■ Zones for quiet and noisy activities.
■ Built-in seating with padding for comfort.
■ A bathroom, a shower, and a whirlpool.
■ Large mirrors, a music system, and a TV for viewing fitness tapes.
■ A well-planned ventilation system.

This well-designed workshop provides built-in dust collection, plenty of cabinets for tools and supplies, and well-planned electrical circuits to get power to the tools without creating a jungle of extension cords.

LAUNDRY/UTILITY ROOMS

You probably have a washer and dryer in your home already, but you might not like their location. Besides, an attic renovation or a basement or bonus room makeover may require (or provide an opportunity for) upgrading your laundry facilities. A complete laundry center should include:

■ Wall cabinets hung out of the way above appliances.

■ Base cabinets with countertops for folding and sorting clothes.

■ A large sink with paper-towel dispenser and storage for rags and cleanup tools.

■ A built-in ironing board.

■ A laundry chute from upper floors.

A sauna fits perfectly with a basement bathroom adjoining an exercise area. Sufficient insulation is a must. A sauna door should not have a latch and should push open easily.

BATHROOMS

One of the first considerations when planning a new bathroom is to determine where the existing plumbing is. You can reduce plumbing costs by putting your new bathroom directly below, above, or back-to-back with an existing bathroom.

Make sure the new bath is large enough. For a master bath, plan the space for two adults and include a shower and a tub, double sinks, and plenty of storage and vanity space.

Plan for easy access, especially to bedrooms. If you can't have direct access from a bedroom, locate the bath just down a hallway. To keep your bathroom private, shield its doorway to prevent direct view from family activity areas.

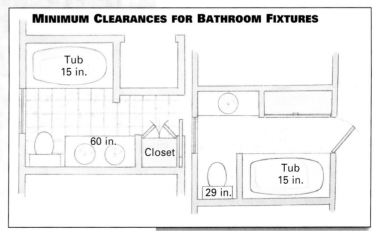

MINIMUM CLEARANCES FOR BATHROOM FIXTURES

Tub 15 in.

60 in.

Closet

29 in.

Tub 15 in.

THE FINISHING TOUCHES

F loor and wallcoverings, window and door trim, and lighting will all affect the look and style of your new room. Also, floor covering and lighting are two major factors that establish the room's comfort and practicality.

FLOOR COVERINGS

You can choose from many materials, styles, and colors of floor covering. Here are some popular floor choices and some factors to consider when you shop for flooring:

WOOD: Wood adds warmth and a feeling of permanence to any room, and it will last a lifetime. If you need a strong linear design in your flooring, install hardwood or manufactured strips or planks. Parquet creates geometric designs.

RESILIENT AND LAMINATE MATERIALS: These sheet and tile materials combine countless design styles with easy installation. Resilients give, so they resist permanent dents; laminates provide a harder surface.

CERAMIC TILE: Tile comes in many sizes, colors, and textures. It is hard and durable. Its weight makes it less suitable for attics, but it can be installed in a bonus room if the floor is strong enough. It's ideal for basements.

Select floor coverings suitable to the uses of your room as well as its overall design. There's a material that will fit every style and budget.

CARPET: Carpet muffles sound and is the most comfortable material underfoot. Sold in many colors, textures, and patterns, carpet will suit any room and any style.

WALLCOVERINGS

Wallboard (drywall)—the most common wall surface found in today's homes—is typically painted. But painting is not the only wallcovering choice available. Wallpaper—alone or combined with paint—presents many decorating possibilities.

STAIR TREATMENTS

Stairways can act as the focal point for your entire design scheme. For added drama, open up the ceiling around the stairs. You'll increase the play of light in the room and create a startling visual effect. If this step is too bold for your tastes or your budget, here are some more conventional treatments:

■ Cover the treads with hardwood or carpeting—or paint them before tacking down a carpet runner in the middle.

■ Replace the single overhead light fixture with wall sconces at the angle of the stairs.

■ Don't leave the walls bare—hang mirrors, a wall decoration, or create display nooks for small sculptures or plants.

A lighting plan is an essential element of design. A window lets in daylight here, and task and accent lighting are both functional and decorative, illuminating work surfaces and enhancing the look of the home office.

MAKING DESIGN DECISIONS

These tips will help you make decisions more easily:
- ■ Large and busy patterns and dark, muted colors make a room seem smaller. Bright colors make a room seem larger.
- ■ Light wall colors add interest to unusual angles. Contrasting colors will make them focal points.
- ■ Vertical patterns make walls seem higher. Horizontal patterns will seem to add width.
- ■ Structural elements can add interest. Leave beams and rafters exposed if they harmonize with other design elements.

WINDOW STYLES

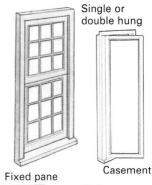

Single or double hung

Casement

Fixed pane

Sliding

Awning

Pick window styles carefully. Match their function, appearance, and materials with the style and uses of your new room conversion.

Walls and ceilings are often textured by either spraying or rolling on heavy-bodied material to make a rough surface. Wood paneling—solid boards or sheet materials—brings warmth and beauty to a room, and its installation (generally over wallboard) requires only basic carpentry tools and skills. Tile is a popular bathroom wallcovering.

Offices, hobby rooms, and other special-purpose rooms often call for something different in wallcovering. For instance, bulletin-board material or perforated hardboard can go in work areas or mirrors can cover one wall of an exercise room.

YOUR LIGHTING PLAN

Well-planned lighting illuminates and enchants a space. Lighting needed for a room includes general illumination, task lighting, and accent lighting. Balancing the three kinds enhances the beauty and usefulness of a room.
- ■ General illumination provides safety and convenience and establishes the overall mood of a room. Choose the location of new windows and indirect lighting fixtures (globe fixtures, recessed ceiling lights, wall sconces, or floor-mounted spotlights) so they provide warm, even light over large areas of the room.
- ■ Task lighting shines on specific work or reading areas. Spotlights, track lights, wall-mounted fluorescent fixtures, lamps, or recessed ceiling fixtures focus the light on desks, countertops, or other activity areas.
- ■ Accent lighting is decorative. Aim recessed ceiling spotlights or sconces at accents—plants, pictures, architectural objects or features of the room—to enhance their effect.

TRIM STYLES

PICTURE FRAME CASING

Mitered corner

Casing

BUTTED HEAD CASING

Butt joint

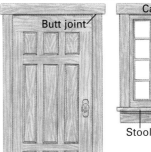

Casing

Stool   Apron

CABINET HEAD CASING

Butt joint

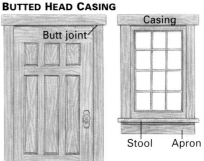

Casing

Stool   Apron

CORNER BLOCK CASING

Head casing

Butt joint

Corner block

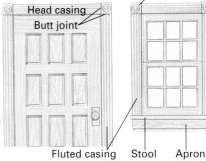

Fluted casing   Stool   Apron

TRIM WORK

Trim and molding hide minor gaps and imperfections at joints and around doors and windows. They also contribute to the style of a room. Some popular moldings:
- ■ Picture-frame molding—with its straight lines and mitered corners—provides a simple complement to modern design schemes.
- ■ Butted-head trim is easy to install and projects an Arts-and-Crafts feeling.
- ■ Cabinet-head casing—a variation of the butted-head style—adds a small trim piece at the top of the casing.
- ■ Corner blocks originated in the Victorian era. Their elaborate designs are well-suited to formal styles.

Trim around doors and windows should match the style of the room.

MAKING YOUR IDEA WORK

IN THIS SECTION

Changing the Space **16**

Improving Access
And Storage **18**

Altering the
Systems **20**

Letting the Light In **22**

Keeping the
Moisture Out **23**

Once you decide to remodel, you'll form a mental picture of how the new room will look. But don't make final plans until you look closely at the attic, basement, or bonus room. You may find problems you hadn't anticipated.

This chapter provides solutions to the most common problems—expanding floor space, raising ceiling height, changing stairways, removing old walls and erecting new ones, and rerouting electrical and plumbing lines.

THE SKELETON OF YOUR HOME

Houses are built in layers, each supported by the one below it. Every structural member does a specific job. Here's how the parts work together in a typical frame house:

FOOTING: A concrete pad that extends into the soil around the slab floor, supporting the floor and the foundation walls.

SLAB FLOOR: Concrete—4 to 6 inches thick—reinforced with wire to resist cracking, that provides a floor surface and supports the foundation walls.

FOUNDATION WALLS: Poured concrete or block wall that carries the weight of the wood frame walls of the upper stories. A mudsill, anchored to the top of the foundation wall, provides a base for the first-story floor.

WOOD FRAME FLOORS: Generally 2× stock, consisting of:

■ **JOISTS:** Members, set on 16-inch centers, that support the subfloor and finished floor materials. At the perimeter, they are called *rim joists* or *band joists*. The ceiling joists of one story are the floor joists of the one above.

■ **BRACING:** Adds strength to joists and keeps them from collapsing.

■ **SUBFLOOR:** Sheet material, usually plywood, that provides a base to attach finished flooring to.

FRAME WALLS: Usually 2×4 or 2×6 lumber, consisting of:

■ **SILL PLATE:** Base for the studs.

■ **STUDS:** Vertical structural members, set on 16-inch centers, that form the wall and support the upper stories. Studs are normally doubled at corners, covered with sheathing and siding on the exterior and finish wall material on the interior.

■ **TOP PLATE:** Horizontal piece that ties studs together at the top of the wall and provides a base for upper stories. It's usually doubled.

■ **HEADER:** Doubled 2× stock above a door or window opening that transfers the weight of the structure above to the walls, away from the door or window.

RAFTERS: Main members of the roof structure that provide support for exterior roof sheathing and roofing material.

RAFTER TIES: Horizontal members that keep the weight of the roof from pushing out and spreading the top of the walls.

TYPICAL FRAMING

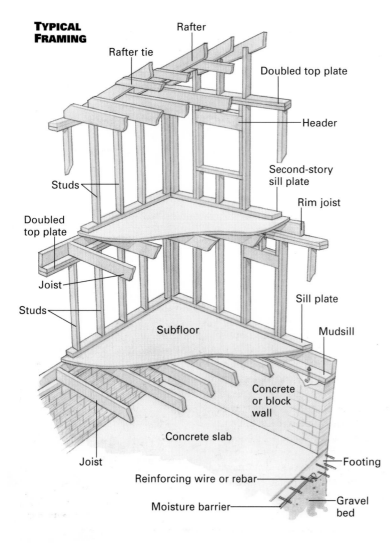

- Rafter
- Rafter tie
- Doubled top plate
- Header
- Second-story sill plate
- Rim joist
- Sill plate
- Mudsill
- Concrete or block wall
- Footing
- Gravel bed
- Studs
- Doubled top plate
- Joist
- Studs
- Subfloor
- Concrete slab
- Joist
- Reinforcing wire or rebar
- Moisture barrier

PLUMBING AND ELECTRICAL SYSTEMS

Plumbing and electrical systems may seem formidable, but in each of them flow proceeds logically from one stage to the next.

PLUMBING WATER SUPPLY SYSTEM:

Fresh water enters and and waste leaves in the following order:

■ **BUFFALO BOX:** Located close to the street, this is the utility supplier's shutoff valve.

■ **MAIN SHUTOFF:** A valve inside (sometimes outside) the house that controls the flow to the entire system. Use it to shut off water when making major repairs to the system or in the absence of supply valves at individual fixtures.

■ **WATER METER:** A device that measures water usage. (Not used on private well systems.)

■ **FIXTURES** Sinks, toilets, and appliances, sometimes controlled by individual stop (shut-off) valves.

PLUMBING DRAIN-WASTE-VENT (DWV) SYSTEM:

Pipes that carry away wastewater and sewer gases.

■ **BRANCH DRAINS:** Wastewater flows through a trap in these pipes to the main drain.

■ **MAIN DRAIN:** Large drain on the lower house level which carries waste to public sewer lines or septic system.

■ **VENT PIPES:** Pipes connected to the branch or main drains and extended through the roof to allow sewer gasses to escape.

ELECTRICAL SYSTEM:

■ **WEATHERHEAD:** Where power from the utility company substation enters your home, generally on three overhead wires. (Some areas have underground electrical lines.)

■ **METER:** Device that measures electricity use.

■ **SERVICE PANEL:** Box which distributes power through circuit breakers into individual circuits which serve outlets, switches, and fixtures in the home.

■ **OUTLETS:** Points for connecting appliances to an electrical circuit.

TYPICAL PLUMBING AND ELECTRICAL SYSTEMS

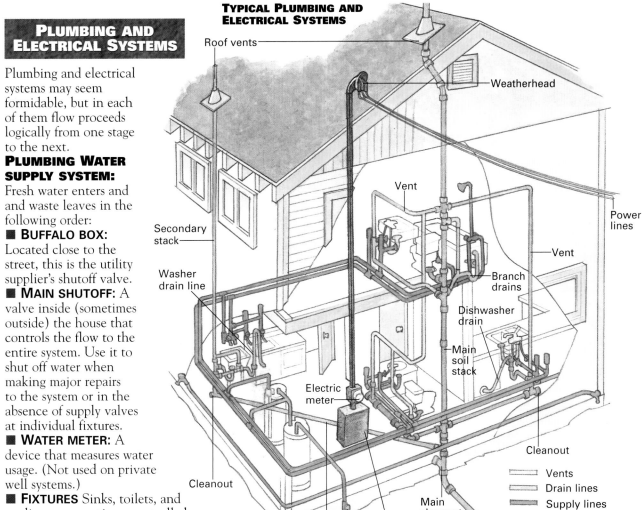

Roof vents — Weatherhead — Power lines — Vent — Branch drains — Dishwasher drain — Main soil stack — Cleanout — Vents — Drain lines — Supply lines — House sewer — Main cleanout — Electrical service panel — Water meter — Main shutoff — Branch drain — Electric meter — Cleanout — Washer drain line — Secondary stack — Vent

TRUSSES

Trusses, factory-made structures of dimension lumber, speed roof construction and cut costs. They also reduce usable attic space and make remodeling virtually impossible. Removal of a truss member can destroy the structural integrity of the entire roof. In some cases, trusses can be modified, but if your roof is built with trusses, don't modify them without consulting a registered engineer.

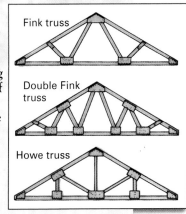

Fink truss

Double Fink truss

Howe truss

CHANGING THE SPACE

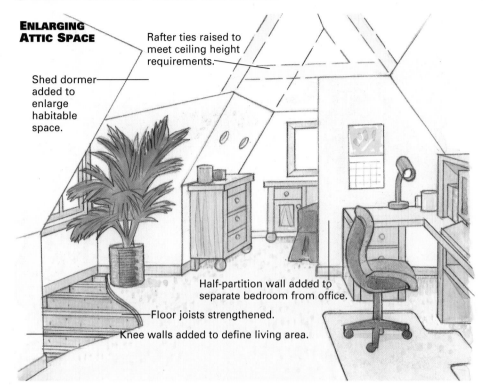

ENLARGING ATTIC SPACE

Rafter ties raised to meet ceiling height requirements.

Shed dormer added to enlarge habitable space.

Half-partition wall added to separate bedroom from office.

Floor joists strengthened.

Knee walls added to define living area.

One of the first problems you may encounter is that the space in your new room won't accommodate the uses you want. Perhaps the ceiling is too low for an attic bedroom. There might not be enough floor area for the power tools you need in your basement workshop. Or maybe the area of that unused back room is cavernous, when all you want is a place to take care of the family bills. Ductwork in the basement might clash with your teenager's sense of style for his or her new bedroom. This section shows a number of techniques you can use to remove or overcome such obstacles.

RAISING ATTIC CEILINGS

An attic ceiling may be high enough down the center, but not over enough of the floor area to meet code requirements for a habitable room. Raising the ceiling enlarges the habitable floor area. Altering the rafter ties or building a dormer are two methods of raising attic ceiling heights. Here's a look at the two methods:

■ Rafter ties keep the weight of the roof from pushing out on the house walls. You can usually remove them as long as you replace them (one at a time) with the ceiling joists.

If you want to leave the rafter ties exposed and they're only 4 to 6 inches too low, you can raise them by that amount (again, replace one tie at a time) without weakening the roof's structure.

The same techniques may work in attics with existing ceilings, but you should consult a structural engineer to make sure the ceiling joists don't function as rafter ties.

■ Adding a dormer to the attic offers two benefits: It raises the ceiling to create more habitable space and it brings in more light from its window. To build a dormer, you'll need to support the existing rafters, cut an opening in the roof, erect walls, roof the dormer, and install a window.

Another way is to raise a portion of the roof. This process calls for similar construction techniques as dormer-building (with the addition of a new ridge beam supporting the raised section), but leaves a portion of the existing roof intact.

INCREASING BASEMENT HEADROOM

Basements usually don't have enough headroom. Even if the floor joists above are at the correct height, pipes and ductwork often

ENLARGING WITHOUT ALTERING

If space in your new room seems small and you can't enlarge it, these techniques will make any room, especially one with a low ceiling, appear larger.

■ Small, light-colored furnishings clustered in groups open up space and make it seem organized.

■ Wall-mounted light fixtures draw attention to the walls, and the spread of horizontal light imparts a sense of depth.

■ Continuous solid-colored flooring or material with an uncomplicated pattern simplify the space.

■ Mirrors are great deceivers. So are curved surfaces. Hang a mirror on a long wall to make the room seem wider. Round off corners—curves don't stop the eye.

■ Room dividers (in place of partition walls) allow sight lines over them, giving the illusion of a larger space.

get in the way. When you survey your basement, see if piping and ducts can be rerouted. (Remember that drain lines must have $\frac{1}{8}$ to $\frac{1}{4}$ inch of fall per linear foot of run.) Rerouted lines between the joists can be hidden behind the new ceiling.

Lowering the basement floor—a more difficult and costly solution— will also increase headroom. This job starts with removal of the slab within the perimeter. To do that, break it up with a sledge or jackhammer. Then you will have to excavate the soil, construct a new footing and wall, and pour a new slab. Seek the advice of a licensed engineer and contractors before you decide on this method to increase basement headroom.

DIGGING NEW DIGS

If you must have additional space in the basement and your budget will withstand the expense, you can add a room by excavating and adding on outside an existing foundation wall. The original foundation wall will then become a partition wall within the expanded basement.

Excavation may prove easier than lowering the slab floor, because you'll be digging in clear space and you won't have to remove the slab from within. Locate the new room under an existing section of the house (in a former crawl space, for example), or you will have to build an addition above it or roof it.

REMOVING WALLS

An existing wall that stands in the way of your new room may be just a minor obstacle. Before planning to remove a wall, however, determine whether it is load-bearing or nonbearing (see page 36). You can remove most nonbearing walls with little difficulty, but removing a bearing wall calls for temporary support walls and a new beam. Some can't be removed at all.

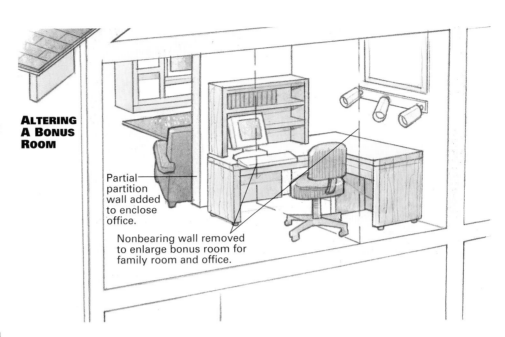

ALTERING A BONUS ROOM

Partial partition wall added to enclose office.

Nonbearing wall removed to enlarge bonus room for family room and office.

ERECTING NEW WALLS

The addition of a new partition wall (or knee walls in an attic) is the easiest way to reconfigure space to meet your needs. Frame walls go up easily and require only basic skills. Concrete block walls in basement rooms are more difficult, and unless your plans include excavation or building codes require them, you probably won't need to use block for a partition wall.

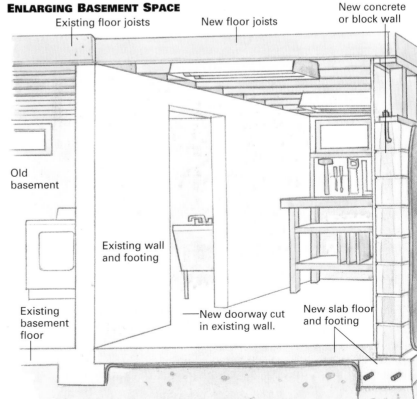

ENLARGING BASEMENT SPACE

Existing floor joists

New floor joists

New concrete or block wall

Old basement

Existing wall and footing

Existing basement floor

New doorway cut in existing wall.

New slab floor and footing

IMPROVING ACCESS AND STORAGE

STAIR SPECIFICATIONS

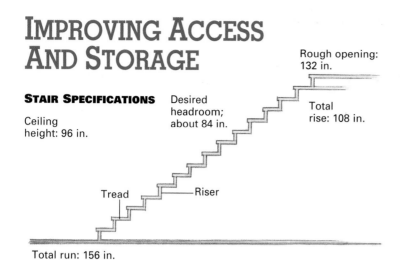

Ceiling height: 96 in.

Desired headroom; about 84 in.

Rough opening: 132 in.

Total rise: 108 in.

Tread

Riser

Total run: 156 in.

IMPROVED STAIR CONSTRUCTION

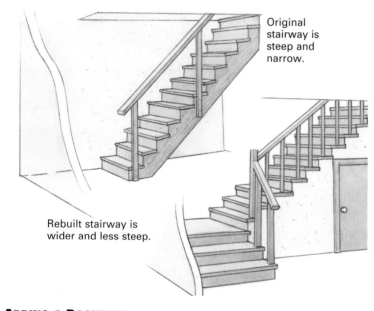

Original stairway is steep and narrow.

Rebuilt stairway is wider and less steep.

ADDING A DOORWAY

Opening cut in basement block wall allows access to new deck.

How you will get in and out of your new room is a major consideration. You should address it early in your planning. You may need to add or change a doorway into a bonus room or alter both the placement and shape of attic and basement stairs to make them safe and convenient.

Changing stairways almost always results in other decisions, because stairs to habitable spaces must meet code requirements for primary stairs, which are different than codes for stairs to nonhabitable space (see code requirements, below).

If your existing stairs aren't suitable for the job, you can do one of these:
■ Rebuild them in the same location.
■ Build new stairs in a different location.
■ Construct a new exterior entry.

LOCATING A NEW STAIRWELL

Even if your present stairway meets code, study its location and style. You may want to change one or more of the following aspects if it doesn't fit your new room design.

HEADROOM: Attic stairs centered under the roof ridge offer the most unobstructed headroom. Basement stairs in older homes are often built under an upper stairway—their headroom is compressed by the upper stringers. You may need to relocate them.

CONVENIENCE: Locate the stairs to a multiple-room attic so family members don't have to pass through a bedroom or a bath to get to the stairs. Stairs leading to family rooms should originate close to the kitchen.

NOISE: Noise travels both up and down staircases. Avoid connecting noisy and quiet rooms, or soundproof the stairwell.

STRUCTURAL SUPPORT: Although a relocated stairway can be built parallel or perpendicular to the joists, a parallel installation requires less cutting, materials, and installation time.

CODES FOR PRIMARY STAIRS

The following are typical requirements for primary stairs.
RISER HEIGHT: 7½ inches maximum
TREAD DEPTH: 9 inches minimum
WIDTH BETWEEN HANDRAILS: 32 inches minimum
HEADROOM: 80 inches minimum
HANDRAIL HEIGHT: 30 to 34 inches above tread

STAIR STYLES

If your present stairs intrude into the space in your new room or their style doesn't suit you, consider other designs. Remember that stairs take a lot more room than they might appear to. A simple straight stairway needs almost 40 square feet of floor area at its lower level. L-shaped, U-shaped, and other stair designs take up even more floor space. If your stairs are cramped for space, a spiral stair or winding stairway may solve the problem.

Spiral stairs are usually 4 to 6 feet in diameter—the perfect size for small lofts and retreats. Moving furniture up or down them is difficult, however, and codes may not allow their installation to upper rooms larger than 400 square feet.

Winders eliminate the need for a landing around a sharp turn. Their construction requires precision, so check with code officials before putting a winder in your plans.

PLANNING STORAGE

Increase storage capacity in your attic, basement, or bonus room with these ideas:

■ Put dead space to work—recess storage under stairs, above crawl spaces, behind knee walls, under eaves, and above ceilings. Most of these areas come with their own architectural quirks and require custom solutions. If knee walls in the attic don't fit your design, use the space to store attractive furniture or other objects.

■ Cover an entire wall with built-in shelving or enclosed cabinets with doors in a style that complements the overall design. Don't build in storage on sections of the wall where furniture will go.

■ Put a lid on enclosed storage bins under windows. Use the lid for informal seating or for plants.

■ Jazz up your closet with ready-made rack dividers, shoe racks, and hanger bars set at different heights.

ALTERNATE STAIR DESIGNS

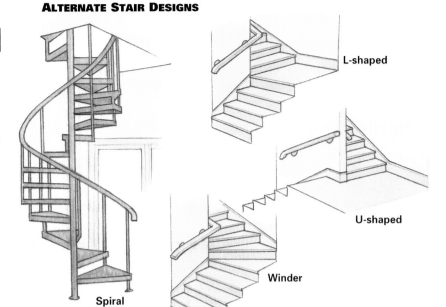

L-shaped

U-shaped

Winder

Spiral

CREATING STORAGE SOLUTIONS

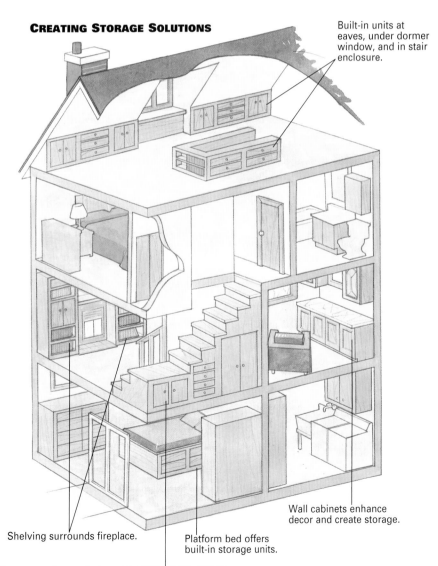

Built-in units at eaves, under dormer window, and in stair enclosure.

Wall cabinets enhance decor and create storage.

Shelving surrounds fireplace.

Platform bed offers built-in storage units.

Turn unused space below stairs into usable storage.

ALTERING THE SYSTEMS

Remodeling will almost certainly require alteration of electrical, plumbing, or heating, ventilating, and air conditioning (HVAC) systems. You may need to run new wiring, plumbing lines, or ducts to a living area.

These alterations will also affect structural work, but you won't have to compromise your room design for most of them—if you include them in your plans at the start.

PLANNING ADEQUATE WIRING

Although you may be tempted to extend existing electrical circuits into your remodeled space, you should install at least one new general-purpose circuit to avoid overloads. Here are some additional guidelines for wiring:

■ Install at least one outlet on each wall more than 2 feet long; place outlets not more than 6 feet from each other.

■ Locate switches close to room entrances.

■ Install separate outlets and circuits for fixed appliances.

■ Give stairways ample lighting and install two-way switches at both ends.

■ Protect basements and bathrooms with a ground-fault-circuit-interrupter (GFCI) outlet. It shuts off power to the circuit immediately when it senses a danger of shock.

■ Relocate existing wiring, but when you reroute (or install new) wiring through studs or joists, observe the precautions about drilling holes (see page 47).

WHERE TO PUT THE PLUMBING?

The ideal location for new plumbing is directly above, below, or back-to-back with existing lines. The next-best option is to conceal pipes in walls, closets, or utility rooms.

If neither of these solutions will work, look for a location in the middle of a lower-story room that will allow you to run the drain pipe horizontally and turn it downward in a closet or other concealed space.

ALTERING ELECTRIC, PLUMBING, AND HEATING SYSTEMS

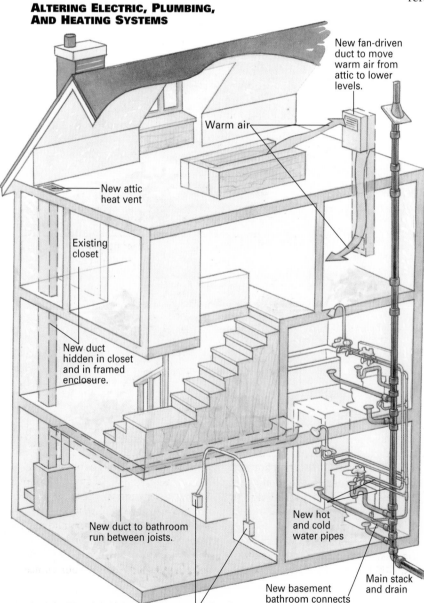

New fan-driven duct to move warm air from attic to lower levels.

Warm air

New attic heat vent

Existing closet

New duct hidden in closet and in framed enclosure.

New duct to bathroom run between joists.

New hot and cold water pipes

Main stack and drain

New basement bathroom connects to main stack.

New outlets installed, wiring rerouted across top of new door to bathroom.

TREES HELP COOL AND HEAT

Landscaping can help keep areas of your house comfortably heated or cooled.

Trees planted on the east side of the house will shade it from the morning sun. West-side plantings will shade the house in the afternoon. Deciduous trees—those that lose their leaves in the winter—will give you shade in the summer but when the leaves are down, they will let in the warming winter rays.

DEALING WITH DRAINS

Joists are usually large enough to allow the necessary fall for drain lines, so running the lines between and parallel to joists may not pose a problem.

If the joists are too small or you can't make a parallel run, hang the pipe below the joist and box it in to conceal it.

In basements, make sure you tap into drains that are large enough. Drains for washing machines and sinks are almost never large enough for a new system. However, a toilet probably drains into a pipe of adequate size.

If the main drainpipe runs through the floor, you can probably tap into it safely, but if it goes into a wall, it may be too high to allow the proper fall. If it's only a few inches above the floor, you can install a toilet or shower on a platform—as long as the ceiling will leave room for the shower stall.

One last option is to install a new branch drain. You'll have to dig up the slab floor and install new fittings, but it will be worth the effort if it's the only way you can install a new basement bathroom.

VENT SOLUTIONS

You can reroute vents in the attic fairly easily—cut them off below floor level, install a 90-degree elbow, run the extension between floor joists to a point beyond the knee wall, and from another elbow, run the vent pipe through the roof. Just make sure all vents extend at least a foot above the roof.

If you're running new vents through existing lower-story rooms, hide them in a partition wall or conceal them in a box. Don't run vents through exterior walls; you're certain to run into horizontal fire blocks, other wiring, window framing, and insulation. Running a vent pipe up the wall on the outside of your house may be allowed in your community. It's easy, but unattractive.

HEATING AND COOLING

Whether forced air, hot water, or steam, HVAC systems can usually handle the extra load of remodeled space. Just run additional ducts or pipes through walls or hide them in other ways. Make sure the capacity of the existing unit will accept the new load. If it won't, you'll probably need to upgrade or install an additional heating or cooling source—electric baseboard or gas heaters, a wood-burning stove, or a room air conditioner. Because cooling is also affected by ventilation, plan windows and skylights so they cross-ventilate the room, and install a ceiling fan if necessary.

INSULATING SAVES ON HEATING AND COOLING COSTS

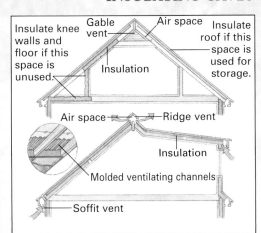

Most bonus rooms will be insulated, but attics and basements may have inadequate insulation.

In your attic, you'll need fiberglass batts, rigid foam (fireproofed by a drywall covering) or fiberglass boards. You'll also need an air space from soffits to a gable or ridge vent.

If your rafters are not deep enough to handle all this material, you can add 2×2 furring or sister new rafters to the old ones.

The most critical area for basement insulation is along the rim joist. Install fiberglass blanket insulation on the inside and rigid foam on the outside. To insulate the interior wall, glue rigid foam between furring strips or hang fiberglass blankets between studs. Insulate a slab floor with 2×4 sleepers and rigid foam between them. Cover the sleepers with plywood underlayment and the finished floor of your choice.

LETTING THE LIGHT IN

BALANCING THE LIGHT

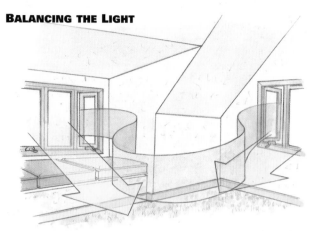

In an attic, basement, or bonus room, windows on adjacent walls will balance the amount of light in all sections of the room and provide cross ventilation.

INCREASING ATTIC LIGHT

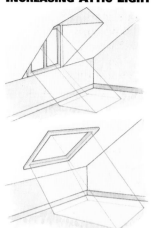

A roof window or skylight lets in up to five times more light than a wall window and is less likely to be obstructed by trees or buildings.

Attics and basements are usually dark. Many attics have only a single gable window, and basement windows are usually small. Bonus rooms may not have enough light because of window placement.

One of your first design goals should be to brighten up the space with additional windows. Here are some factors to consider:

BALANCE THE LIGHT: Natural light should enter a room from more than one direction. In basements and spare rooms, place windows on different walls. In attics, use windows and skylights, or put skylights on opposite slopes of the roof.

AVOID OVERHEATING: East-facing windows will get the morning sun. West-facing openings will gain heat in the afternoon. Reduce overheating with opaque or bronzed glazing.

HEAT LOSS: To minimize heat loss, install the best thermal windows that your budget will allow. Removable insulating panels for windows will reduce heat loss too.

VIEWS: Windows should open to pleasant views, even if it means changing the layout of the room. Keep upper-story views at or above the horizon, and take privacy—both yours and your neighbors'—into account.

TIPS FOR BASEMENT WINDOWS

DOWNSLOPE WINDOWS: Any wall with most of its exterior above grade provides a suitable location for a large window; add as large a unit as you can. Place the bottom frame as close to ground level as possible. Install glass doors where possible.

CLUSTER SMALL WINDOWS: If no wall is big enough for a large window, cluster small windows to let in the light.

BUILD A LARGE WINDOW WELL: You can install a picture window in a below-grade wall by excavating an area and building a large-scale window well (left). You can make an entrance by adding steps and installing a sliding glass door instead of a window. Decorate the well with plantings, or terrace the retaining wall to create a garden spot outside the window or door.

BUILDING AN EXCAVATED ENTRANCE WELL

CODES FOR LIGHT AND VENTILATION

Window area in a habitable room must be at least 8 percent of the floor area. Unless mechanical ventilation is provided, 50 percent of the glazed area must be openable.

KEEPING THE MOISTURE OUT

Moisture is one of the major enemies of home construction, and its potential problems aren't limited to basements. Before you get too far along with your plans, inspect your home for evidence of moisture. Fix problems before you start remodeling.

SLEUTHING IN THE ATTIC

Even if you don't have an obvious leak, water can still come through the roof and cause rot. Inspect your attic on a bright day, armed with a screwdriver. Look closely at the sheathing for water stains. Poke suspect areas and look for matted insulation. Look also for pinholes of light shining through the roof. Poke around the edges of vents, chimneys, and skylights—sealing or flashing can often loosen. If you find trouble, you may be able to patch things up, but water damage often means you need a new roof.

MOISTURE IN THE BASEMENT

Basement moisture can be caused by condensation, leaks, and hydrostatic pressure, which forces moisture up through the floor. Each problem has its own cure.

CONDENSATION: Condensation shows up on walls and cold water pipes in warm weather. To prevent these surfaces from collecting water from the moist summer air, insulate pipes and walls and cover wall insulation with a vapor barrier. Adding windows to increase ventilation will help. So will a dehumidifier, but don't rely on it solely.

LEAKS: if your basement leaks, first make sure gutters and downspouts are installed and in good repair. Many problems can also be solved by grading the soil around the house away from the foundation. If these remedies don't work, you may have to invest in an exterior or interior drainage system (see illustration at right).

HYDROSTATIC PRESSURE: White deposits (alkali) on the slab means you might have a moisture problem. To check for moisture, tape 2×2-foot squares of clear plastic to the floor every 2 feet. Lift them after a couple of days. Water droplets under the plastic mean moisture is wicking up through the floor from the soil, and you may need to consult with an engineer for solutions.

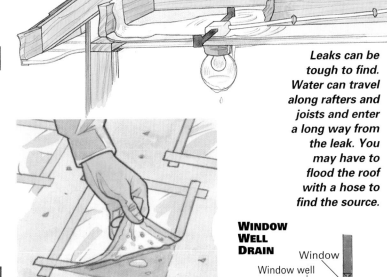

Leaks can be tough to find. Water can travel along rafters and joists and enter a long way from the leak. You may have to flood the roof with a hose to find the source.

Tape poly film to the floor. Water droplets may indicate the need for a new drainage system.

To keep water from collecting in a window well and seeping inside, line the base with concrete and install a drain.

WINDOW WELL DRAIN

Window
Window well
Surface drain
Gravel
Perimeter drain
Drain to dry well

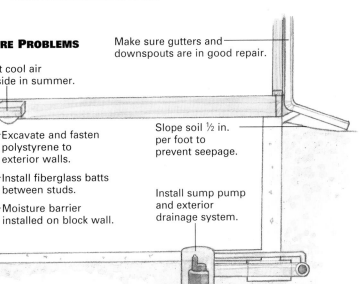

SOLVING MOISTURE PROBLEMS

Vent cool air outside in summer.

Make sure gutters and downspouts are in good repair.

Excavate and fasten polystyrene to exterior walls.

Install fiberglass batts between studs.

Moisture barrier installed on block wall.

Slope soil ½ in. per foot to prevent seepage.

Install sump pump and exterior drainage system.

Persistent leaking, puddles, or flooding need immediate attention. Waterproofing the interior walls and sealing the cracks with hydraulic cement will sometimes cure these problems. Better yet, waterproof the exterior walls, and install a sump pump and drain lines that run to a dry well.

MAKING PLANS

Project planning starts with conversation and ends on paper. Detailed plans will save you time, effort, and money.

IN THIS SECTION

*Build Within
Your Budget* **25**
Drawing Plans **26**
*Do It Yourself
Or Hire a Pro?* **28**

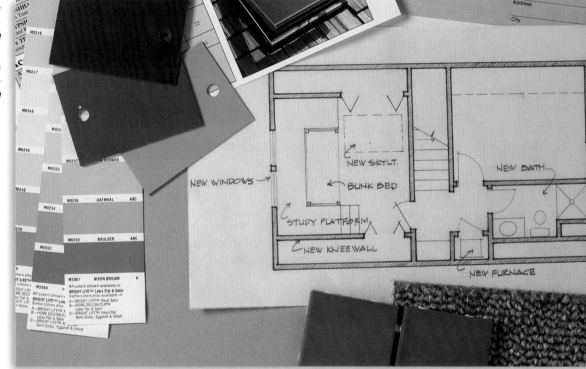

Careful planning is essential to a successful remodeling project. Now is the time to take out wish lists, paint chips, design ideas, and rough sketches and put your dream on paper.

You'll need to make some lists too: materials estimates, construction and inspection calendars, and—if you contract out some of the work—a bidding and contracting schedule.

All this effort will pay off in both the short and the long run. If you do the job yourself, these plans and lists will be your guide. Even if you end up contracting the work, detailed plans will provide a lot of answers and save time and money later. Professionals estimate at least a third of any remodeling project involves planning. It lays the groundwork for everything else and is the key to making the project exciting and enjoyable.

PLANNING CHECKLIST

Use this checklist to organize your project from start to finish:
■ Measure the room carefully and calculate its area.
■ Create a scaled drawing that includes all dimensions and design peculiarities.
■ Using the area of the room, estimate material quantities—structural lumber, fasteners, underlayments, and finish materials.
■ Estimate your total costs and comparison-shop for the best deals.
■ Prepare a calendar that includes your construction schedule, contract benchmarks, and when inspections will be conducted.

BUILD WITHIN YOUR BUDGET

Be specific—that's the watchword for successful planning. Make detailed plans and you'll know ahead of time how the room will turn out. Make final decisions during planning about how you will use your room and what will go in it.

If you want comfortable seating when watching TV, elbowroom for exercise, or space to show off your wine collection and keep its temperature controlled, make those decisions before building begins. Then you'll know how to set up the space—how large the open area should be, the dimensions of closets and cabinets, and the arrangement of furnishings and lighting. Include these details on your floor plan.

HOW MUCH WILL IT COST?

This is the first thing people want to know when planning a remodeling project. The answer depends on the size of the project, its complexity, and the quality of materials.

With detailed plans, suppliers or contractors can provide accurate cost estimates. If the estimates are higher than expected, detailed plans will help you decide exactly how to substitute cost-saving measures and be certain they won't destroy the usefulness or enjoyment of the space. Make changes during the design phase; changes made after the contractor has begun the work (called *change orders*) usually increase costs. Sometimes, changes require undoing or redoing work that's already been completed, which increases costs considerably.

KEEPING THE WORK IN ORDER

Remodeling comes with its own construction order. Sticking to it will keep you out of trouble; include the steps below on your construction calendar:
- Fix moisture problems
- Reroute ductwork and surface-mounted pipes and cables; move drainpipes
- Install windows
- Remove walls
- Frame partition walls
- Rough in stairs
- Rough in HVAC, DWV, and supply lines
- Rough in electric lines
- Insulate exterior walls
- Hang ceiling drywall
- Hang drywall on walls, tape joints
- Prime drywall
- Paint room
- Lay finished floor
- Trim doors and windows and install cabinets

HOW MUCH CAN I AFFORD?

This is the second—and more important—question. You probably won't find the answer by simply glancing at your checkbook. Remodeling an attic, basement, or bonus room is not an inexpensive undertaking, and for most homeowners it will require some kind of loan from a financial institution.

You may not know how much you can borrow until you actually apply for a loan. Gather financial data ahead of time. Make a list of current debts and payment amounts, figure your net worth, and list any anticipated new expenses (and income) that you will have during the life of the loan. Doing this ahead of time will speed your application.

COMBAT CONFUSION

One aspect of planning won't lend itself to graph paper and a ruler—the inevitable disruption and mess caused by remodeling. Somehow, no matter how well-planned the project, water gets turned off at the wrong time, the plastic sheet blows off the exterior window opening in the rain, or you can't get to the basement because the stairway isn't completed.

Here are a few things you can do to minimize the stress of remodeling:
- Clear out the work area. Sell unwanted items at a garage sale and reorganize what you're keeping. Start doing this several weeks before you begin the project.

- Anticipate debris disposal. Collect sturdy cartons for hauling out plaster or drywall pieces. Rent a trash container to collect debris, and make a chute for easy removal of debris from upper-story demolition.
- Order materials early; have all preparations completed by the delivery date.
- Buy tarps to cover materials that will be stored outside.
- Make sure you have the right tools—or know where to rent them—before you start work. Nothing slows a project—or dampens your enthusiasm for it—like stopping to search for a tool.

- If possible, isolate the rest of the home from the project area. Tape plastic over the doorways to contain dust. If the kitchen is closed, make alternate arrangements for meals. Keep at least one bedroom available so you can get away from it all.
- Choose the right season. Spring and summer are better times to cut through outside walls, but moderate fall weather may be better for working in an attic.
- Above all, leave yourself plenty of time. Do things in a logical order. Refer to "Keeping the Work in Order" (above) and allow sufficient time for each stage.

DRAWING PLANS

Whether or not you intend to do all the work yourself, planning on paper will help you make sure the finished work looks exactly as you have imagined it. Planning starts with measurements and a dimensioned drawing, which begins with a rough sketch of the room.

MAKING A DIMENSIONED DRAWING

First, make a rough sketch of the contours of the room, identifying appliances, closets, nooks and crannies, and cabinets and other built-in features (even if you plan to remove them). Then measure everything exactly. Start in a corner and measure the length of a surface from each change of direction to the next. Measure the location and opening size of existing windows and doors precisely. Note the measurements on your sketch.

ATTIC FLOOR PLAN

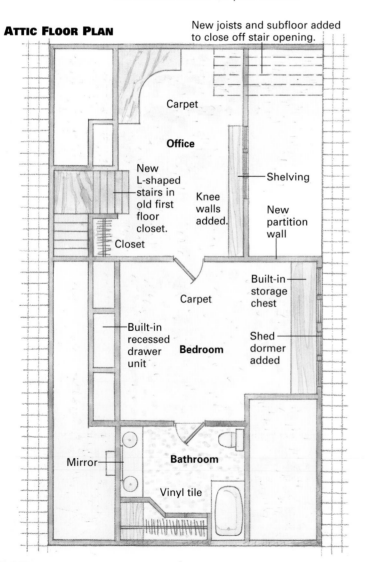

New joists and subfloor added to close off stair opening.

Carpet

Office

New L-shaped stairs in old first floor closet.

Closet

Knee walls added.

Shelving

New partition wall

Carpet

Built-in storage chest

Built-in recessed drawer unit

Bedroom

Shed dormer added

Mirror

Bathroom

Vinyl tile

DESIGN PROFESSIONALS CAN SAVE YOU MONEY

Even if your budget is tight, hiring a design professional is often worthwhile. A designer can incorporate ideas you've seen in other homes, conceptualize design schemes, draw plans, and advise you about changes that will make your project more efficient and less expensive. Professional design help is available from several sources:
■ Architects are trained in building design and engineering. They are qualified to advise you on structural requirements.
■ Interior designers are trained to plan and style interior space.
■ Design/build firms often have staff architects or designers, and can carry out your project from start to finish.

Now transfer the sketch and all its details and irregularities to graph paper. Use a scale that's comfortable (¼ inch=1 foot is convenient). Then write in the measurements you've taken.

This should give you an accurate rendering of the space as it now exists. What you need next is a "picture"—several, actually—of the proposed structural and other changes you will make. You'll use tracing paper for these.

THE FLOOR PLAN

Tape a piece of tracing paper to your dimensioned drawing and trace those elements of the old room that will remain in the new one. Leave out (or draw with dotted lines) elements you will remove—a wall, for example. Draw in any new framing details—doors, windows, walls, dormers—and label

DRAFTING TOOLS

Making a dimensioned drawing will, like any other endeavor, be easier if you have the right tools. Here's what you need:
■ Graph paper with a scale of ¼ inch=1 foot
■ Several sizes of drafting triangles
■ Circle templates
■ Templates for furnishings
■ Pencils, sharpener, and erasers
■ Several sheets of tracing paper

them. When you're done, your drawing will look something like the floor plan illustrated at right. If something doesn't look like you had imagined it, modify the floor plan until you are satisfied with it. This is the time to experiment with changes. If you experiment on tracing paper, it's easy to change—you'll avoid erasing the drawing and starting over.

Although the floor plan reflects what your new room will look like, it's not detailed enough to serve as a guide to build from. You will need several additional drawings that show more detail—a construction or framing plan, and similar renditions for electrical, plumbing, and HVAC systems. You can trace these detailed plans yourself, hire a professional designer, or leave it to a contractor. In any case, you can get materials estimates based on the information in your floor plan.

PREPARING FOR ESTIMATES

List the dimensions of the room on a copy of your new floor plan, and compute the total area of the room. Rooms that don't have built-in features are easy. Simply multiply their length by their width. In rooms with odd spaces and closets, you will have to compute the area of the individual sections and add them to get the total. In still others, it will be easier to multiply the longest dimensions together and subtract the area occupied by permanent features.

Now make a complete list of materials and take it and the floor plan to your materials dealer. The supplier will be able to provide you with a reasonably accurate estimate of material costs.

Your set of detailed plans should show where to stub in any plumbing work. Lay out drainpipes first. Make precise measurements.

BASEMENT FLOOR PLAN

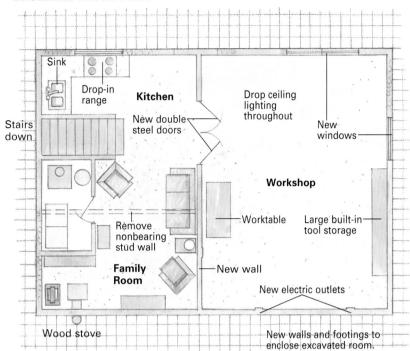

TYPICAL FIXTURE ROUGH-IN DIMENSIONS

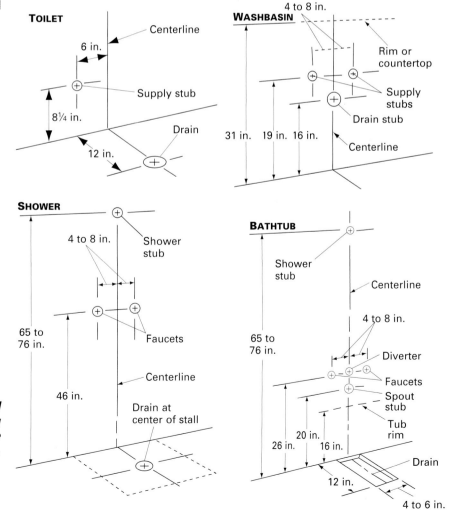

DO IT YOURSELF OR HIRE A PRO?

Whether you do the work yourself or hire a contractor, planning always pays off. Detailed plans will make you familiar with the project and help you negotiate a reasonable cost.

If you are an experienced do-it-yourselfer, you probably plan to tackle your remodeling project. If you're still undecided about contracting some or all of the job, the following guidelines will help you decide.

WILL I SAVE MONEY?

Doing the work yourself will almost always save you money if you don't put monetary value on your time, and if the work will not cause lost time and income from your occupation. Contracted remodeling will cost roughly two to two-and-a-half times more than the cost of materials—plus additional interest on this amount if you take out a loan. Even if you decide to contract the work, you can save money if you:

■ Do the work of the most costly pros—the plumbing and electrical work, for example. Make sure your local codes allow this.

■ Perform tasks that have high labor/low materials cost, such as demolition, excavation, insulating, and drywall finishing.

■ Do small jobs that would take a contractor less than half a day to finish, such as installing resilient sheet or manufactured wood flooring.

■ Select, order, purchase, and arrange material delivery yourself.

DO-IT-YOURSELF QUESTIONNAIRE

Once you've passed the cost hurdle, there are a few other questions that will help clarify your do-it-yourself decision.

■ Your skills and time. Are you experienced in home improvement work? Do you possess the carpentry, electrical, and plumbing skills this project will demand? Do you have the proper tools, or access to them? Do you enjoy working on your home? Do you have the time—and the patience—to stay with the job, even if it remains unfinished for several months? If you answered yes to these questions, you should consider doing the job yourself. If you answered no to most of them, consider acting as your own general contractor or contracting out the entire job.

■ Management. Are you well organized, persistent, and clear about your goals? Can you spend long hours on the telephone and on the job site? Can you handle money, make payments promptly, and stay on budget? Are you comfortable negotiating with subcontractors and suppliers? If you answered yes to most of these questions, you should consider being your own general contractor. If you answered no to these questions and to the skills-and-time questions above, then you probably should contract the job out.

HOW TO FIND A CONTRACTOR

First of all, you need to hire a licensed general contractor—someone who meets state requirements for all the work your project calls for. General contractors have a broad knowledge in all areas of construction. Your general contractor will probably hire subcontractors—licensed individuals with expertise in a specific area of work—electrical, carpentry, or plumbing, for example.

DO YOU WANT TO BE A GENERAL?

Acting as the general contractor for the job can be a satisfying and cost-saving way of completing your remodeling project. A general contractor hires professional tradespeople and supervises their work.

As a general contractor, you will have important responsibilities and you will also be expected to do certain things. Here are some of the duties of a general contractor:

■ Be thoroughly familiar with your plans and subcontractors. Workers will expect you to know what you want and be able to communicate it clearly.

■ Make all payments to your subcontractors promptly and in the amount invoiced.

■ Be cooperative, but stay out of the way.

■ Maintain accurate work schedules. If your job is not ready when the subcontractor arrives, the subcontractor may not be able to return for some time because of other scheduled work. Keep everyone on the schedule informed of possible delays.

Start your search for a contractor with your friends, neighbors, and professional acquaintances. Ask them for the names of firms that did work for them that they were satisfied with. Get six to eight names.

Meet with each contractor and discuss your project. Show your floor plans and other drawings you have made. Don't hesitate to ask the contractor about experience with similar conversions. Also ask for a rough estimate of the project cost. This estimate is not binding; it's a quick way to determine how well the contractor knows the work you want and how comfortable the builder is in discussing costs.

Ask for evidence of bonding, a certificate of insurance, and references. A bond insures that the work will be completed if for some reason your contractor fails to complete the job. Insurance protects you if someone is injured while working on your property.

Pay attention to your instincts during this meeting. Contractors and clients have to get along—sometimes for extended periods—and you want to choose someone with whom you can work comfortably.

BIDDING THE JOB

After meeting with each contractor, narrow your list to four or five and request bids from them. Give each one the same amount of time to respond—three weeks should be enough. Eliminate bids that come in late without good reason.

Study the bids carefully. Here's what to look for:

■ Itemized materials lists (including quantities and brand names of major appliances or fixtures) along with labor costs.
■ A timeline for scheduled completions specifying the amount to be paid for each stage of completed work.
■ Costs for change orders—modifications you make to the job after the work has started.
■ The amount of the contractor's fee.

Be suspicious of bids that vary substantially from the average. The lowest bid—and the highest one—will not always guarantee the lowest cost or best results.

SIGNING THE CONTRACT

When you've selected your contractor, you should sign a written agreement that addresses all of the following concerns:
■ Description of work to be completed by the contractor and subcontractors and a calendar listing completion dates and payment amounts for each stage of the project. This schedule should allow for delays due to inclement weather, late material deliveries, and material back orders, and should reference floor plans and any other constructions drawings.
■ Description of materials, including model numbers or specifications/styles of major elements, such as cabinetry.
■ Right of rescission clause, giving you the right to back out if you change your mind.
■ Statement that the contractor is responsible for securing building permits and scheduling inspections.
■ Name of bonding authority and certificate of insurance.
■ Warranty guaranteeing quality of materials and labor for at least one year.
■ Procedures for approving change orders.
■ Mechanic's lien waivers. These guarantee that subcontractors and suppliers will not put liens on your property if they are not paid by the contractor for work.
■ Final walk-through and approval. When the job is done, you and your contractor should take a complete walk-through of the work and note anything you are not satisfied with. Your contract should allow the contractor a reasonably short amount of time to remedy such problems.

CALENDAR OF INSPECTIONS

Job	Work to Be Checked	Time of Inspection
Foundation	Trench, forms, rebar	Before concrete is poured
Under the floor	Floor, framing, utility lines	Before subfloor is installed
Framing	Grade of lumber, connections	Before sheathing is applied
Sheathing	Seams, nailing patterns	Before roofing or siding
Rough plumbing	Pipe sizes, materials	Before plumbing is covered
Rough wiring	Wire sizes, boxes, workmanship	Before wiring is covered
Roofing	Materials, flashing	After roofing is completed
Energy efficiency	Insulation, window area	Before applying wallboard
Interior walls	Wallboard nailing pattern	Before taping and mudding
Flues/fireplace	Clearances, materials	Before covering
Gas line	Fittings, pressure test	Before covering
Final inspection	Electrical fixtures, plumbing fixtures, railings, furnace smoke detectors	After completion

CONSTRUCTION BASICS

Your design is finished, the plans are drawn, and you have the permits in your pocket. Now you're ready to begin tearing out the old room and building the new one.

In most cases, demolition will be the first thing to do, followed by structural changes specific to your plans. This chapter describes general techniques you'll use to build the structure of your room.

These techniques apply to all projects; they are not specific to an attic, bonus room, or basement. Later chapters will show you how to apply them to your specific project.

IN THIS SECTION

Floor Basics	**32**
Wall Basics	**36**
Door and Window Basics	**40**
Stair Basics	**44**
Wiring Basics	**46**
Plumbing Basics	**48**

Remodeling requires knowledge of construction basics such as building walls, whether your new room is in the attic, basement, or bonus room.

Using the right fastener is one of the keys to proper construction. Here's some information to help you choose the correct ones.

FASTENERS FOR FRAMING

Framing fasteners come in a variety of forms—nails, screws, lag screws, bolts, and metal framing connectors.

NAILS hold things together by the friction they generate against wood fibers. Their size is determined by length expressed as pennyweight, abbreviated as *d*.
■ Common nails, used for general construction, have large heads for greater holding power.
■ Box nails, thinner than their common cousins, reduce splitting in ¾-inch or thinner stock.
■ Finishing nails have tapered heads, which allow them to be countersunk in interior trim.
■ Casing nails are used in place of finishing nails where more strength is needed.
■ Drywall nails have slightly cupped heads, which dent the surface of drywall.
■ Ringshank and spiral shank nails increase holding power in flooring materials.

SCREWS work because their threads create tension within the wood fibers. You'll find wood screws with oval, round, and flat heads. Here are some used for construction work.
■ Bugle-head (or wallboard) screws are threaded from the head to a sharp point and have a head designed for countersinking.
■ Decking screws, the galvanized or rustproofed version of drywall screws, have thicker shanks for holding larger framing.

LAG SCREWS are larger than conventional screws, have a hex or square head, and are used to hold large framing members together.

BOLTS have nuts on one end, and hold parts together by compressing their surfaces.
■ Machine bolts have a hex or square head.
■ Carriage bolts have a rounded head for a decorative or finished appearance.

FRAMING CONNECTORS are designed for a number of special purposes.

FRAMING FASTENERS

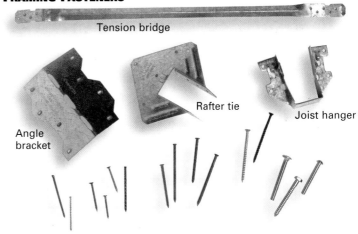

Tension bridge

Rafter tie

Joist hanger

Angle bracket

- Joist hangers make joist installation easier and stronger.
- Rafter ties connect rafters to top plates.
- Tension bridges add lateral strength to floor and ceiling joists.
- Angle brackets add strength to perpendicular joints—at rim joists and stair stringers, for example.

MASONRY FASTENERS

Masonry fasteners are similar to nails or screws. Some are hardened and others rely on expansion and friction to grip masonry.

MASONRY NAILS are hardened steel with squared edges and a rough surface that binds to concrete.

ANCHOR BOLTS have a band at their base which expands when you tighten it. They are used to fasten framing members to concrete walls or slabs.

EXPANSION SHIELDS slip into holes drilled in the masonry. The metal shields expand to grip the hole when a lag screw is driven in.

WALL ANCHORS are similar to expansion shields, with flanges, toggles, or flaring plastic tips that grip the interior surface of the mounting hole.

MASONRY FASTENERS

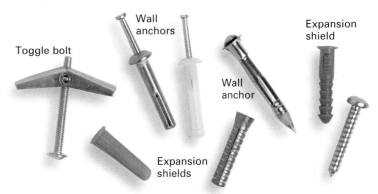

Wall anchors

Toggle bolt

Expansion shield

Wall anchor

Expansion shields

BEWARE OF LEAD AND ASBESTOS

Lead oxides were used in paints up to about 30 years ago to speed application and improve durability. Lead was also used for plumbing through the early 1900s and in solder for copper pipes. Unfortunately, lead is a toxin that can be ingested if released into the air or drinking water.

Asbestos contains fibers that are now known to be carcinogenic. It was used as a binding material in resilient flooring installed before 1986 and in various forms of insulation, ceiling finishes, and shingles.

Removing either material can pose an extreme health hazard. Take the following precautions if you find either in your home:
- Remove all lead plumbing.
- Replace, paint over, or otherwise cover surfaces known to contain lead paint—don't strip them. Never use a sander of any kind or a torch on paint suspected of containing lead. Call 1-800-424-LEAD for advice on lead paint removal.
- Don't attempt removal of any material that you suspect contains asbestos; disturbing the material will disperse fibers into the air. Cover resilient floor material rather than ripping it up. Contact a professional asbestos abatement contractor for removal. Call 1-800-638-CPSC (the Consumer Products Safety Commission) for more information about asbestos hazards.

WORKING SAFELY

From demolition to finish, remodeling can expose you to certain dangers. Always keep the work space safe and dress for safety.
- Clutter (including unneeded tools) is distracting and potentially dangerous. Remove demolition debris as you go. Plan the work in stages and bring only the tools you need to the work area.
- Boots and leather gloves prevent cuts and scratches and will give you a better grip.
- Wear a dust mask or respirator. Change the filter often.
- Wear knee pads for comfort and to prevent injury.
- Don't forget to put on safety glasses. The ones with windows at the temples maintain peripheral vision while protecting your eyes.

FLOOR BASICS

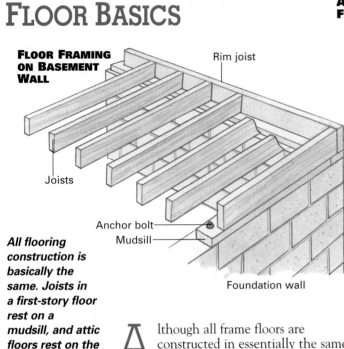

FLOOR FRAMING ON BASEMENT WALL

Rim joist

Joists

Anchor bolt

Mudsill

Foundation wall

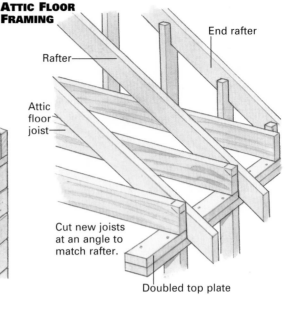

ATTIC FLOOR FRAMING

End rafter

Rafter

Attic floor joist

Cut new joists at an angle to match rafter.

Doubled top plate

All flooring construction is basically the same. Joists in a first-story floor rest on a mudsill, and attic floors rest on the double top plate of the wall below. You may need to cut off the corners of new attic joists to accommodate the rafter angle.

Although all frame floors are constructed in essentially the same way, slight differences exist in how first- and upper-story floors are supported on the mudsill and top plates. Before making modifications, note the differences shown in the illustration above.

IS THE FLOOR STRONG ENOUGH?

Even if your remodeled room has an existing floor, it may not be strong enough for its new use. Attic joists, especially, may be sized only for ceiling and storage loads and may need strengthening if you're converting attic space to living space. The floor in your first-story spare room may be strong enough for general family use, but may need shoring up if you're installing ceramic tile. Most local codes have strict requirements for joist material and span, but you can get a rough idea of what you need by using the span tables below.

First, measure the span of the joists and their on-center spacing. Then check one of the span tables below to see what size joists are required for the use of the room. For example, for a sleeping room, 2×4 Douglas fir joists graded "select structural" and spaced 12 inches on center can span a distance of 12 feet, 6 inches. The same lumber set on 16-inch centers can only span a floor of 11 feet, 4 inches.

Note also that the specifications depend on the use of the room—heavier loads of

FLOOR JOISTS IN SLEEPING ROOMS AND ATTICS: 30 PSF LIVE, 10 PSF DEAD

Species Group	Spacing in O.C.	2×4				2×6				2×8				2×10			
		Sel. Str.	No.1	No.2	No.3	Sel. Str.	No.1	No.2	No.3	Sel. Str.	No.1	No.2	No.3	Sel. Str.	No.1	No.2	No.3
Douglas Fir- Larch	12	12-6	12-0	11-10	9-8	16-6	15-10	15-7	12-4	21-0	20-3	19-10	15-0	25-7	24-8	23-0	17-5
	16	11-4	10-11	10-9	8-5	15-0	14-5	14-1	10-8	19-1	18-5	17-2	13-0	23-3	21-4	19-11	15-1
	19.2	10-8	10-4	10-1	7-8	14-1	13-7	12-10	9-9	18-0	16-9	15-8	11-10	21-10	19-6	18-3	13-9
	24	9-11	9-7	9-1	6-10	13-1	12-4	11-6	8-8	16-8	15-0	14-1	10-7	20-3	17-5	16-3	12-4
Hem-Fir	12	11-10	11-7	11-0	9-8	15-7	15-3	14-6	12-4	19-10	19-5	18-6	15-0	24-2	23-7	22-6	17-5
	16	10-9	10-6	10-0	8-5	14-2	13-10	13-2	10-8	18-0	17-8	16-10	13-0	21-11	20-9	19-8	15-1
	19.2	10-1	9-10	9-5	7-8	13-4	13-0	12-5	9-9	17-0	16-4	15-6	11-10	20-8	19-0	17-11	13-9
	24	9-4	9-2	8-9	6-10	12-4	12-0	11-4	8-8	15-9	14-8	13-10	10-7	19-2	17-0	16-1	12-4
Southern Pine	12	12-3	12-0	11-10	10-3	16-2	15-10	15-7	13-3	20-8	20-3	19-10	15-8	25-1	24-8	24-2	18-8
	16	11-2	10-11	10-9	9-0	14-8	14-5	14-2	11-6	18-9	18-5	18-0	13-7	22-10	22-5	21-1	16-2
	19.2	10-6	10-4	10-1	8-3	13-10	13-7	13-4	10-6	17-8	17-4	16-5	12-5	21-6	21-1	19-3	14-9
	24	9-9	9-7	9-4	7-4	12-10	12-7	12-4	9-5	16-5	16-1	14-8	11-1	19-11	19-6	17-2	13-2

JOIST REPAIRS AND ADDITIONS—BASEMENTS AND ATTICS

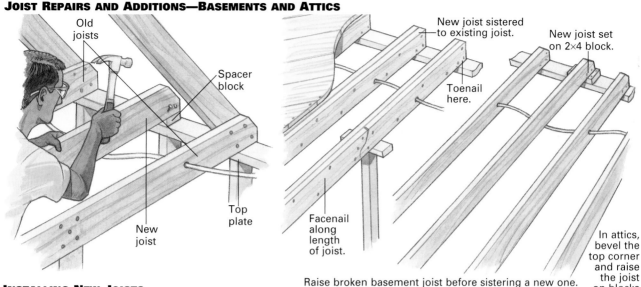

INSTALLING NEW JOISTS

Raise broken basement joist before sistering a new one.

EXTENDING JOISTS

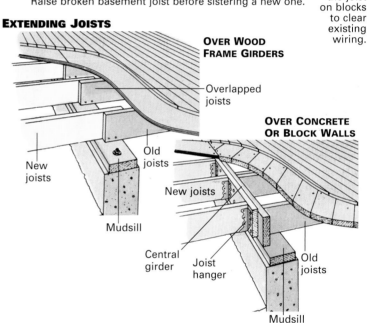

common living spaces reduce the allowable span. Requirements also change if joists are ceiling joists only and don't support living-space floor loads. Check requirements with your building code official.

STRENGTHENING A FLOOR

If you find that your floor won't meet code, you can strengthen it by adding larger joists, or *sistering* additional joists to the old ones. Larger joists added to a floor become the new support structure—they replace the old joists, although you will leave the old ones in place. Sistering joists with lumber of the same size doubles the joist thickness. Both remedies may require altering existing wiring and plumbing.

FLOOR JOISTS IN ALL ROOMS EXCEPT SLEEPING ROOMS AND ATTICS: 40 PSF LIVE, 10 PSF DEAD

Species Group	Spacing in O.C.	2×4				2×6				2×8				2×10			
		Sel. Str.	No.1	No.2	No.3	Sel. Str.	No.1	No.2	No.3	Sel. Str.	No.1	No.2	No.3	Sel. Str.	No.1	No.2	No.3
Douglas Fir-Larch	12	11-4	10-11	10-9	8-8	15-0	14-5	14-2	11-0	19-1	18-5	17-9	13-5	23-3	22-0	20-7	15-7
	16	10-4	9-11	9-9	7-6	13-7	13-1	12-7	9-6	17-4	16-5	15-5	11-8	21-1	19-1	17-10	13-6
	19.2	9-8	9-4	9-1	6-10	12-10	12-4	11-6	8-8	16-4	15-0	14-1	10-7	19-10	17-5	16-3	12-4
	24	9-0	8-8	8-1	6-2	11-11	11-0	10-3	7-9	15-2	13-5	12-7	9-6	18-5	15-7	14-7	11-0
Hem-Fir	12	10-9	10-6	10-0	8-8	14-2	13-10	13-2	11-0	18-0	17-8	16-10	13-5	21-11	21-6	20-4	15-7
	16	9-9	9-6	9-1	7-6	12-10	12-7	12-0	9-6	16-5	16-0	15-2	11-8	19-11	18-7	17-7	13-6
	19.2	9-2	9-0	8-7	6-10	12-1	11-10	11-3	8-8	15-5	14-8	13-10	10-7	18-9	17-0	16-1	12-4
	24	8-6	8-4	7-11	6-2	11-3	10-9	10-2	7-9	14-4	13-1	12-5	9-6	17-5	15-2	14-4	11-0
Southern Pine	12	11-2	10-11	10-9	9-4	14-8	14-5	14-2	11-11	18-9	18-5	18-0	14-0	22-10	22-5	21-9	16-8
	16	10-2	9-11	9-9	8-1	13-4	13-1	12-10	10-3	17-0	16-9	16-1	12-2	20-9	20-4	18-10	14-6
	19.2	9-6	9-4	9-2	7-4	12-7	12-4	12-1	9-5	16-0	15-9	14-8	11-1	19-6	19-2	17-2	13-2
	24	8-10	8-8	8-6	6-7	11-8	11-5	11-0	8-5	14-11	14-7	13-1	9-11	18-1	17-5	15-5	11-10

FLOOR BASICS
continued

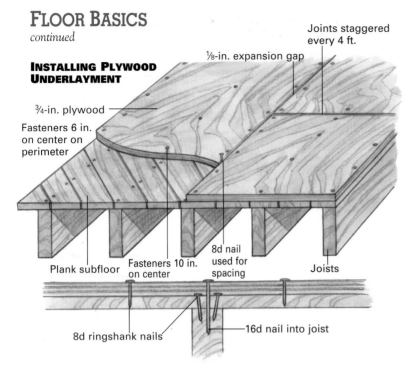

INSTALLING PLYWOOD UNDERLAYMENT

Joints staggered every 4 ft.

1/8-in. expansion gap

3/4-in. plywood

Fasteners 6 in. on center on perimeter

Plank subfloor

Fasteners 10 in. on center

8d nail used for spacing

Joists

8d ringshank nails

16d nail into joist

ringshank nails at 6-inch intervals on the perimeter and 10-inch intervals within the panel. To eliminate squeaks, lay a bead of construction adhesive before nailing. Nail subsequent sheets in the same manner—always perpendicular to the joists and leaving a 1/8-inch expansion gap between them. Use an 8d nail for a spacing guide. When you get to the second course, stagger the joints every 4 feet and cut panels at the ends when a full sheet won't fit. Continue these procedures until you have covered the entire floor area.

REPAIRING THE SURFACE OF A CONCRETE SLAB

If your concrete floor shows no signs of moisture problems, is level (no high spots of more than 1/8 inch in 10 feet) and is not severely cracked, it may need only surface repairs before installing underlayment or the finished flooring. Check the surface for evenness by rotating a 6-foot level on it in sections, marking any defects with a carpenter's pencil. Then repair problem areas, following these steps:

CRACKS AND HOLES: Key minor cracks or holes with a chisel, clean them out, and fill them with a quick-setting hydraulic cement.

LOWS AND HIGHS: Fill depressions with patching compound, feathering it to the surrounding floor. Grind minor high spots down with a rented concrete grinder. If extensive leveling and smoothing are required, consider using liquid underlayment.

ALKALINE SALT DEPOSITS: Alkaline deposits will impair adhesive bonding on glued-down floors. Remove them by mopping the surface with a solution of 4 parts water and 1 part muriatic acid. Then rinse the slab with clean water. Muriatic acid is extremely caustic. Follow directions carefully.

If the slab is slick or sealed and the finished flooring requires an adhesive, roughen the slab by sanding it or scarifying with rented equipment. Then scrub it with degreaser or

INSTALLING A NEW SUBFLOOR

Subfloors—in addition to contributing to the overall strength of the floor—provide a solid base for the finished flooring material. Plywood is the usual subflooring material. It can be used over wood joists or concrete slabs.

Sold in 4×8-foot (and larger) sheets and made of an odd number of thin wood veneers glued together under pressure, plywood resists warping, buckling, twisting, and splitting.

CDX plywood from 5/8 to 3/4 inch thick is the best subfloor for most finished floors. Use PTS (plugged and sanded) plywood or 1/4- to 3/8-inch lauan plywood under resilient sheet or tile flooring.

Beginning at one edge of the room, lay down plywood sheets loosely as a working surface. Line up the first sheet perpendicular to the joists, square to the room, and with its edge centered on a joist. Fasten it with 8d

REPAIRING A CONCRETE SLAB

Key minor cracks (enlarge them at the back) and fill with hydraulic cement.

Break out damaged areas and fill low spots.

Level high spots with a carbide grinder wheel.

Roughen surface if necessary.

LEVELING A SLAB WITH LIQUID UNDERLAYMENT

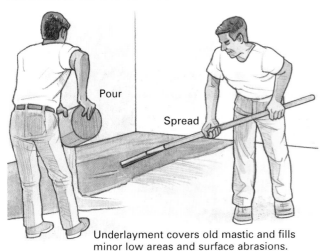

Pour

Spread

Underlayment covers old mastic and fills minor low areas and surface abrasions.

POURING A NEW SLAB OVER AN OLD ONE

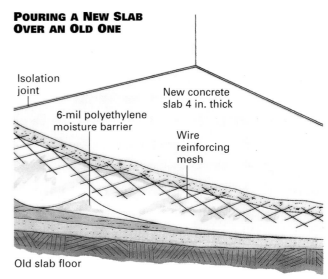

Isolation joint

6-mil polyethylene moisture barrier

New concrete slab 4 in. thick

Wire reinforcing mesh

Old slab floor

a tri-sodium-phosphate solution and hot water. Rinse with clear water and let it dry.

RESURFACING A SLAB

A cracked, broken, or severely damaged slab may not have to be replaced. If its substructure is basically sound and the slab has stopped settling, it may just need a new surface. Before applying either of the surfaces described below, have a structural engineer determine the cause of the current damage. Unstable soil, high water tables, or a shifting foundation call for more involved repair procedures.

SELF-LEVELING COMPOUND: Level a sloped, rough, but structurally sound floor with one of several liquid mortar products. You can buy them from a concrete supplier or at a construction materials store.

Most products require a primer—apply it one day before the compound. After the primer has cured, mix the compound, pour it onto the floor, and spread it out—up to ½-inch thick—with a squeegee. The compound levels itself and dries to a hard, smooth, and water-resistant surface without troweling. If you're using it to bring part of the floor level with another, you can feather it to blend it with the area that's already level. If you need to build up more than ½ inch, add aggregate.

POURING A NEW SLAB: Even if the slab is not structurally sound, you may be able to pour a new floor over the old one, if the resulting

increase in floor height leaves you enough headroom. First install any new plumbing and lay a waterproof membrane over the slab, overlapping its edges by at least 4 inches.

Then lay ½-inch rigid foam around the perimeter as an expansion joint and suspend 6×6-inch no. 10 wire reinforcing mesh on brick or pieces of block to center the wire in the concrete when it's poured. Next, pour in 4 inches of concrete, screed it on the isolation joints, and finish it with a float.

BOXING IN OBSTRUCTIONS

Top plate

Bottom plate

Furnace duct

Cripple

2×2 cross pieces

Pipes and ducts running along the ceiling can pose design and space problems in any remodeling project. Sometimes you can get them out of your way by rerouting them. Or you can hide them above a suspended ceiling. If neither of these solutions will work, make the pipes or ducts part of the design by boxing them in.

Measure the obstruction and build a 2×2 frame to fit. Fasten the frame to the ceiling joists with 3-inch drive screws. Finish the frame with the same materials as the remainder of the room.

WALL BASICS

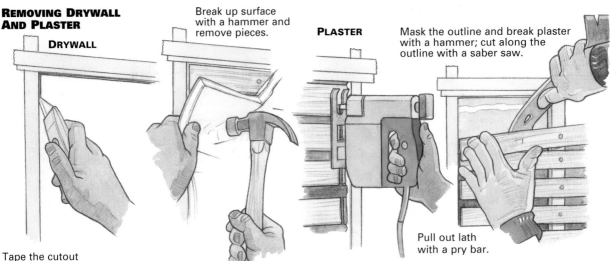

REMOVING DRYWALL AND PLASTER

DRYWALL

Break up surface with a hammer and remove pieces.

PLASTER

Mask the outline and break plaster with a hammer; cut along the outline with a saber saw.

Pull out lath with a pry bar.

Tape the cutout so the cut will be centered on a stud; cut through drywall with a utility knife.

Remodeling almost always requires some modification of at least one wall, ranging from installing a new electric circuit box to cutting an opening for a door or window. In either case, you have to start by removing the drywall or lath and plaster.

CUT THE POWER

Before starting any demolition or repair work on a wall, make sure you have turned off the power to any fixtures on it or wires running through it.

If there is a an outlet or switch box on the wall, turn off the breaker that controls the power to it. Then test the outlet or switch with a circuit tester to make sure the power is off—sometimes two circuits send power to a single box.

Even if no fixture is present, there could still be wiring running through the wall. Look in the attic or basement to see if wiring enters from above or below.

REMOVING THE FINISH MATERIAL

Both drywall and plaster come away easily with simple tools. First, measure around the area to be removed and mark the outline with a carpenter's pencil. Then follow the instructions in the illustration

above to remove the surface material. Taping the outline of the opening will help prevent the material from chipping as you remove it. Don't use too much force when breaking the surface with a hammer. Vibrations transmitted through the framing can cause or enlarge cracks in the surrounding surface or in an adjacent room.

REMOVING A NONBEARING WALL

Before removing any wall, make sure you know whether it's nonbearing or load-bearing. The illustration below left offers some clues to look for, but if you're not certain, call in a professional builder.

Here are some demolition tips:
- Seal off the room to prevent dust from drifting into other areas of the house. Protect the floor with a tarp.
- Save trim for future use. Pry it off gently and pound the nails from the front to avoid splitting the wood.

TYPICAL LOAD-BEARING WALL CONSTRUCTION

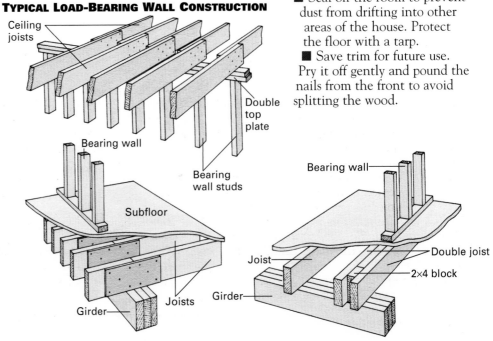

Ceiling joists

Double top plate

Bearing wall

Bearing wall studs

Subfloor

Joists

Girder

Bearing wall

Joist

Girder

Double joist

2×4 block

REMOVING A NONBEARING WALL

■ Save the studs, too. Remove toenailing with a cat's paw or cut through bottom plate nails with a reciprocating saw.
■ Reroute plumbing and wiring before or after removing the wall, depending on the nature of your project.

REMOVING A BEARING WALL

Removing bearing walls requires placement of temporary support walls before demolition. After you have removed the wall, install a beam to keep the upper floor from sagging

3. Twist loose stud off top plate.

4. Pry off sill and top plates; remove nails.

1. Remove covering of adjacent wall back to nearest studs.

2. Knock bottom of stud loose with sledge.

REMOVING A LOAD-BEARING WALL

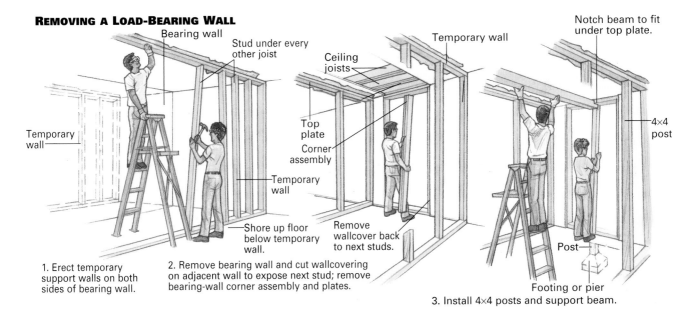

Bearing wall

Stud under every other joist

Temporary wall

Temporary wall

Temporary wall

1. Erect temporary support walls on both sides of bearing wall.

Shore up floor below temporary wall.

Ceiling joists

Top plate

Corner assembly

Remove wallcover back to next studs.

2. Remove bearing wall and cut wallcovering on adjacent wall to expose next stud; remove bearing-wall corner assembly and plates.

Temporary wall

Notch beam to fit under top plate.

4×4 post

Post

Footing or pier

3. Install 4×4 posts and support beam.

or even falling in. Follow the directions in the illustration. Here are some more tips:
■ Prepare the room and remove trim as you would for a nonbearing wall.
■ Temporary support walls are required even when cutting an opening for a window or door. They run the full length and will usually be required on both sides (in both rooms) of an interior bearing wall.
■ "Bearing" means it supports weight all the way to the basement. Shore up the lower floor before beginning and support the new end posts down to the foundation.
■ If you are replacing the wall with a beam, leave the cap plate—the one fastened to the ceiling joists—in place.
■ Pick the correct beam size—consult a pro to make sure it will support the weight on it.

CODES FOR WALL FRAMING

■ Double top plates on load-bearing walls and overlap them at corners, intersections, and joints (by at least 4 feet at joints).
■ Unless the top plate is 2×6, 3×4, or tripled stock, install joists and rafters within 5 inches of bearing studs if the joists or rafters are spaced at more than 16 inches and the studs are spaced on 24-inch centers.
■ Nonbearing partition wall studs may be 2×3s, 24 inches on center or 2×4s, 16 inches on center, and may have a single top plate.
■ Studs may be notched 25 percent of width if bearing and 40 percent if nonbearing.
■ Studs may be drilled 40 percent of width if ⅝ inch or more from edge. Doubled studs may be drilled 60 percent of width.
■ Add fire-stops to walls at top and bottom.

WALL BASICS
continued

TYPICAL STUD WALL

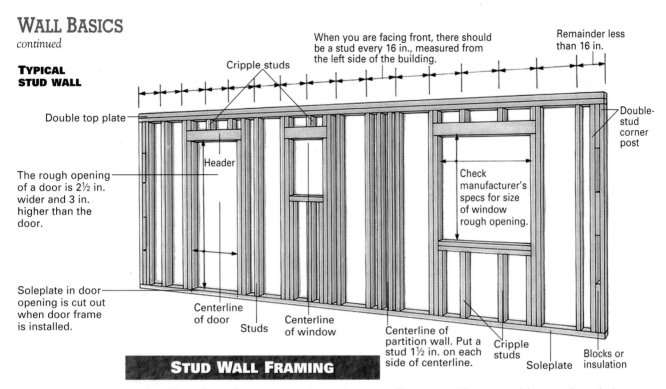

When you are facing front, there should be a stud every 16 in., measured from the left side of the building.

Remainder less than 16 in.

Cripple studs

Double top plate

Header

The rough opening of a door is 2½ in. wider and 3 in. higher than the door.

Double-stud corner post

Check manufacturer's specs for size of window rough opening.

Soleplate in door opening is cut out when door frame is installed.

Centerline of door

Studs

Centerline of window

Centerline of partition wall. Put a stud 1½ in. on each side of centerline.

Cripple studs

Soleplate

Blocks or insulation

STUD WALL FRAMING

Stud walls include these structural members:
STUDS: Usually 2×4s but often 2×6s in new homes, centered at either 16 or 24 inches. Use 2×6s if the wall will support two floors, and space load-bearing studs at 16 inches.

BUILDING AN ASSEMBLED FRAME WALL

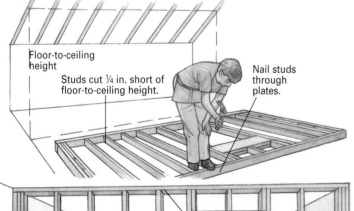

Floor-to-ceiling height

Studs cut ¼ in. short of floor-to-ceiling height.

Nail studs through plates.

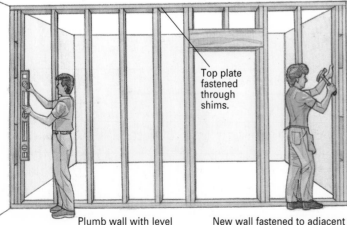

Top plate fastened through shims.

Plumb wall with level before attaching.

New wall fastened to adjacent wall stud or blocking.

PLATES: The top and bottom boards (same size as the studs). Top plates are single in a nonbearing wall and doubled in bearing walls. The top board is called the cap plate.

DOOR AND WINDOW OPENINGS:
Framing for an opening includes:
■ **HEADER:** The top support, usually doubled 2× stock with ½-inch plywood spacers.
■ **JACK STUD:** Supports the header and attaches at the side to a king stud.
■ **SILL:** The bottom of an opening.
■ **CRIPPLE STUDS:** Fill in above and below.

PREASSEMBLY STEPS

Before building a partition wall, strip off the sidewall covering so you can fasten your new wall to the studs. Add horizontal blocking if the new wall falls between studs. You don't have to expose ceiling joists for a nonbearing

WALL TIPS

■ Figure one stud for every lineal foot. Use extras for blocking and cripple studs.
■ Use kiln-dried lumber for door and window openings, pressure-treated lumber for sills on slabs.
■ Build corner posts first and make openings as you go. Cut doorsill after the wall is up.
■ Work in 16-foot sections spiked together after they're in place.

partition wall, unless you're removing the ceiling. Block the ceiling joists if necessary.

BUILDING AN ASSEMBLED WALL

This method will save you assembly time:

■ Lay out and mark the wall location on the floor and ceiling and perform the preassembly steps on the previous page.

■ Cut the plates to length and mark them for studs. Cut the studs ¼-inch shorter than the wall height so the new wall will clear the joists when you raise it. Drill the studs for wiring if you know where it will go.

■ Nail the studs through the plates.

■ Tilt the assembly up on the marks on the floor. Shim the gap at the ceiling, and fasten the plates to the ceiling and floor, plumbing the wall with a 4-foot level.

BUILDING A FRAME WALL IN PLACE

This method is useful when you don't have enough space on the floor to preassemble the wall or when an existing ceiling makes it impossible to tilt a wall into place.

■ First, mark the ceiling or the ceiling joists for the exact location of the top plate. Your ceiling marks should be at joist locations.

■ Measure and cut the plates to length. Mark stud centers on both plates at the same time.

■ Fasten the top plate to the ceiling or joists and drop a plumb bob to mark the location of the bottom plate.

■ Nail the bottom plate to the floor.

■ Measure the length of each stud separately. Studs in a nonbearing wall are generally 3 inches shorter than the wall height, but stud length may vary slightly. Drill the studs for wiring if you're sure of its path.

■ Slide the studs in at the marks and toenail them into place, plumbing them with a level.

BUILDING A BLOCK WALL

Most room remodeling projects will not require a concrete block wall. However, local building codes or construction of a new basement room might require one. Working with block takes patience and stamina. Careful layout is essential.

■ Start by excavating and pouring a footing that meets local code requirements. Embed vertical rebar in the footing every 24 inches.

BUILDING A FRAME WALL IN PLACE

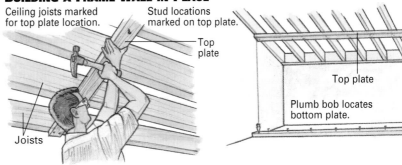

Ceiling joists marked for top plate location.
Stud locations marked on top plate.
Top plate
Joists
Top plate
Plumb bob locates bottom plate.

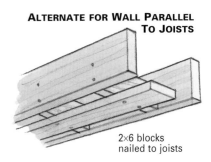

Measure and cut each stud; plumb with level.

In basement, anchor bottom plate with masonry fasteners.

ALTERNATE FOR WALL PARALLEL TO JOISTS

2×6 blocks nailed to joists

■ When the footing has cured (3 days to a week) snap a chalk line to mark the front edge of the wall. Then lay a dry run of blocks spaced ⅜ inch apart.

■ Starting with a corner block, lay the first course in a ½-inch mortar bed. Butter the end of each block and tap it into place. Scrape off excess mortar as you go and adjust the blocks so each is plumb and level.

■ Build corners to four courses and fill in between. Repeat the process until you reach the final height.

BUILDING A BLOCK WALL

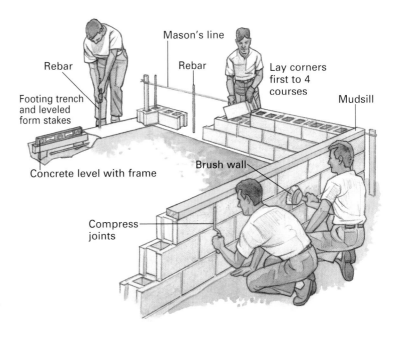

Rebar
Mason's line
Rebar
Lay corners first to 4 courses
Mudsill
Footing trench and leveled form stakes
Brush wall
Concrete level with frame
Compress joints

DOOR AND WINDOW BASICS

Door and window installations used to be jobs strictly for the pros, but the average do-it-yourselfer can install modern windows and prehung doors easily.

FRAMING THE ROUGH OPENING

To frame the rough opening for a door or window, follow the procedures outlined below, referring to the illustration below left and the frame wall shown on page 38.

■ On an existing wall, outline the rough opening (½ to ¾ inch larger than the door or window frame). Make reference marks about 3 feet beyond the outline, because when you remove the wallcovering back to the nearest studs, you'll remove the outline also. The reference marks enable you to locate the edge of the opening again. Measure from the reference marks to the outline and write down the measurement.

If you're making the opening in a new frame wall, mark the center of the opening on the top and bottom plates. From those points, measure and mark the sides of the opening, where the inner faces of the jack studs go.

■ Remove any trim or wallcovering within this outline (see "Removing Drywall and Plaster," page 36) and carefully expand the opening to the nearest studs on either side.

■ If cutting or removing a load-bearing wall, erect temporary support walls. Remove studs within the opening (see page 37).

■ On an existing wall, measure from your reference marks to a point 1½ inches away from the location of the opening. Toenail the king studs at these marks.

On a new frame wall, fasten the king studs 1½ inches outside the marks for the jack studs.

■ Cut jack studs to length and fasten them to the king studs with 16d nails. Cut the header stock to length and assemble its two halves with ½-inch plywood spacers.

CUTTING A ROUGH OPENING

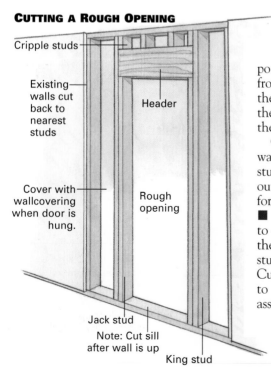

Cripple studs

Existing walls cut back to nearest studs

Header

Cover with wallcovering when door is hung.

Rough opening

Jack stud

Note: Cut sill after wall is up

King stud

DOOR SIZING

■ Exterior doors are typically 1¾×36×80 inches, hinged on three 4-inch hinges.
■ Interior doors are normally 1⅜ inches thick and 80 inches tall, hinged with two 3½-inch hinges. Widths vary from about 16 to 36 inches, depending on use.
■ Doors are either right- or left-handed, depending on the direction they swing from their hinges.
■ Door-jamb width equals the combined thickness of the studs and finished wall material—usually 4⅝ inches for interior walls, 5⅛ inches for exterior ones. When framing a new door or window opening, the rough-opening size is the critical dimension. Make sure you know this dimension before cutting or building the opening.

■ Position the header on the jack studs and fasten it by toenailing and nailing through the king studs.

■ If the opening is for a window, cut and fasten the outer cripple studs (for sill support) and nail them to the jack studs. Toenail the sill to the jack studs.

■ Install any remaining cripple studs.

■ On an existing wall, pound nails at the corners of the opening through the covering or sheathing on the other side; use the nail holes as guides to remove the covering.

■ Replace any necessary wallcovering and remove the sill plate at the bottom of the door opening, if necessary.

INSTALLING A PREHUNG DOOR

Most prehung units come assembled with jambs and stops and the door already hung on its hinges.

Exterior doors have either fixed-width jambs or adjustable-width split jambs. Both install in the same fashion. So do interior doors, except they don't require a sill.

■ First, frame the rough opening using the procedures outlined above or fasten the new frame wall in place (rough opening included, of course).

■ Next, on an exterior door, staple or tack 15-pound felt paper around the bottom, sides, and top of the door opening, overlapping the upper strips over lower ones.

Prepare the door, if necessary, by nailing any unassembled parts into place, cutting extensions above the jamb to fit the height of the rough opening, and cutting excess hinge-screw lengths so they won't catch on the studs. If the unit requires assembly, leave the door unhinged until the casing is in place. If everything is strapped or braced together, don't undo that packing until you have the unit shimmed and nailed.

■ Set the unit in the rough opening and center it. If your model has split jambs, pull them out even with the wall thickness.

■ Insert shims in pairs—one from the inside and one from the outside—to fill the gap between the jamb and framing.

■ Make sure the unit is centered in the frame and drive a 12d finishing nail through the top shims. Plumb the hinge jamb with a level and nail it through the remaining shims.

■ Level the head jamb and nail it.

■ Measure the jamb at the top to make sure the door will shut. Adjust the shims if necessary and nail through the top shims on the latch jamb. Continue checking your measurement as you nail the remaining shims.

■ Score the shims along the jambs and snap them off with a hammer. Install the door hardware and trim.

INSTALLING POCKET DOORS

Pocket door frames come ready-made or adjustable (which don't include the door). Plan the location of either style so the latch will close at an existing stud. In either case, remove wallboard back to the nearest stud and frame the rough opening ½ inch wider and higher than the completed unit.

For a ready-made unit:

■ Set the pocket frame into the rough opening, then plumb and fasten it. Install side and head jambs and screw the track into place.

■ Mount the wheels on top of the door and hook them into the track. Adjust the wheels until the door hangs straight. Finish and trim.

To install an adjustable unit:

■ Adjust the track so both ends are snug against the trimmer studs. Center and level it into the opening.

■ Snap chalk lines on the floor at the outer edges of the studs. Extend both the split jamb and split stud to the chalk lines and fasten them to the track and the floor.

■ Mount the wheel assemblies on the door and hang ththe correct height.

■ Install the door guides and bumper according to the manufacturer's directions. Finish and trim the walls.

HANGING A PREHUNG DOOR

Flashing paper (on exterior wall)

Mitered trim

Casing

Jamb extends flush to thickness of siding.

Stud

Shims

5 pairs of shims on each side.

Jamb secured to frame through shims.

INSTALLING A POCKET DOOR

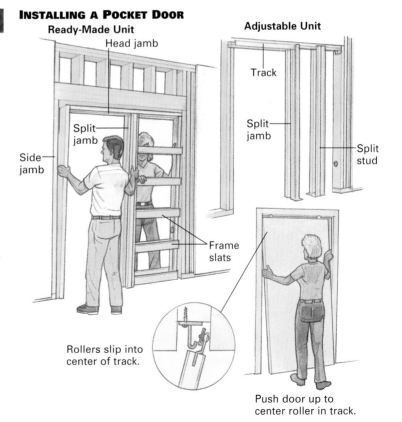

Ready-Made Unit

Head jamb

Split jamb

Side jamb

Adjustable Unit

Track

Split jamb

Split stud

Frame slats

Rollers slip into center of track.

Push door up to center roller in track.

DOOR AND WINDOW BASICS
continued

REMOVING A WOOD FRAME WINDOW

2. With a hacksaw or reciprocating saw, cut the nails that attach the jambs to the studs, then pry the casing away from the exterior wall.

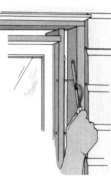

3. Pull the window down and out.

1. Remove the interior casings and stool to uncover the framing. On a large window, cut the sash cords and remove the weights.

REMOVING A WINDOW

Removal techniques are slightly different for wood or metal windows. Removing a wood window involves cutting the jamb nails and removing the unit. Metal frame windows are nailed or screwed to the exterior sheathing through metal flanges. Getting at the fasteners requires cutting the siding.

Follow the directions illustrated on this page, and keep this advice in mind:

■ Measure the rough-opening dimensions before ordering a replacement; strip away the trim to measure it. Tack the trim back in place until you have the new unit.

■ Don't reuse an old double-hung unit; it will allow a lot of heat to escape. Replace the old window with a new, double-glazed window and fill the counterweight channel with polyurethane foam insulation.

REMOVING A METAL FRAME WINDOW

Chalk line 1¾ in. from window frame

Flange

Cut away siding with a circular saw to expose window flange.

CODES FOR WINDOWS

Tempered glass or safety glass is required when the bottom edge of a window is less than18 inches above the floor, its top edge is more than 36 inches above the floor, and its area is greater than 9 square feet. Louvered windows and jalousies with smooth-edge slats at least ¹/₁₆ inch thick and no more than 48 inches long are exempt from the requirement.

SKYLIGHTS: A skylight is any transparent or translucent glazing installed at a slope of 15 or more degrees from vertical. Skylights must be glazed with one of the following:

■ Laminated glass
■ Tempered glass
■ Heat-strengthened glass
■ Wired glass
■ Rigid plastic

TESTING AND CERTIFICATION:
Manufactured windows must be tested and certified to comply with industry standards. (Look for certification label on the window.) The National Fenestration Rating Council (NFRC) rates windows, doors, and skylights for energy performance. Ratings on the NFRC label allow direct comparisons.

■ The opening will probably not be square. Measure it twice across several lengths of the opening before ordering the replacement unit.
■ Order the largest unit that will fit squarely in the opening—with room for the shims, for centering. You can make the opening smaller by nailing 1× or 2× stock to the studs, but then you'll have to change the trim size or modify the interior or exterior wall surface.

INSTALLING A NEW WINDOW

In new construction, windows are installed after the sheathing and before the siding. Installing a window in an existing wall is different, and follows these steps:
■ Prepare the opening. First, measure the diagonals of the rough opening. They should be the same, or within ¼ inch of each other. If they're not, adjust the framing. Make sure the sill is level. Trim the sheathing flush to the edges of the opening.
■ Install window flashing. Two layers of 12-inch wide, 15-pound felt paper can be used as window flashing. Staple the flashing on, as shown at right, overlapping upper pieces over the lower ones. Trim it flush with the studs.
■ If your window comes without a preformed flashing at the top, cut Z-flashing to the required width and slide it under the siding. This flashing must extend about ½ inch beyond the edges at the top of the window.
■ If your window unit comes with brick mold—thick exterior casing trim—cut back the siding so the brick mold fits snugly against it. If your unit does not include casing, build out the jamb until it's flush with the siding to provide a nailing surface for the trim.

Follow the same procedures to replace a window in an existing wall. Slide the flashing paper under the siding.

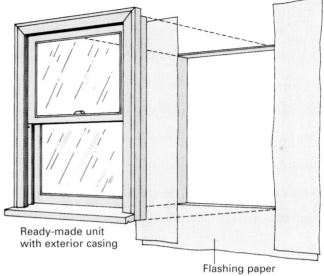

Ready-made unit with exterior casing

Flashing paper

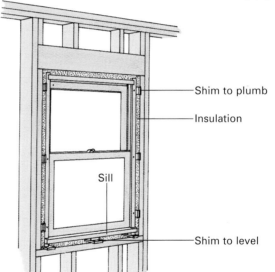

Shim to plumb

Insulation

Sill

Shim to level

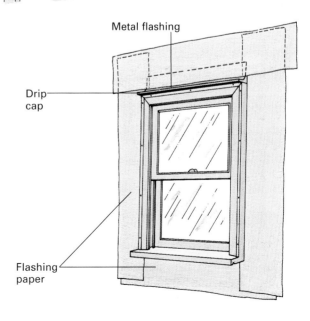

Metal flashing

Drip cap

Flashing paper

WINDOW MATERIALS

Windows are manufactured from many materials. Here are some things to keep in mind when purchasing windows.
■ A wood exterior requires painting about every four years.
■ The wood used in windows is generally a select grade and—whether painted or stained—can add warmth to any room.
■ Solid vinyl—although less expensive—usually performs as well and lasts as long as any other window material.
■ Any window with aluminum in the frame should have an effective thermal break to avoid condensation problems and heat loss.

STAIR BASICS

Building a new stairway is exacting work. It requires planning, patience, and precision. Stair building starts with some math calculations to determine the dimensions of the treads and risers. The total height the stairway climbs (the rise) and its total length (the run) are the key dimensions.

THE MATH OF RISE AND RUN

Calculating stair dimensions comes down to figuring out how many steps you need to get up to the next floor in the horizontal distance available. Here's how to figure stairs:

■ Measure the distance from the lower floor to the surface of the upper floor. This is the total distance the stairs must climb—the rise. It's 8 feet, 2 inches in the example shown.

■ Divide the rise by 7½ inches—an arbitrary figure that represents the average riser height.

The result is the approximate number of steps needed to climb the height. In our example, that's 98÷7.5=13.07. (8 feet, 2 inches=98 inches.) Round the result up to the nearest whole number—in this case, 14.

■ Divide the rise by the rounded number. The result should be between 7 and 8. This is the actual height of each riser. In our example, it would be 7 inches (98÷14=7).

■ Divide the total run by one less than the number of steps—the final step is the upper floor. This calculation gives the tread depth. In our example, it's 10½ inches (136½÷13=10½). Use the riser height and tread depth to lay out and notch the stringers.

FIGURING THE RISE AND THE RUN

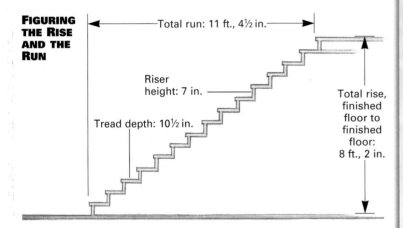

Total run: 11 ft., 4½ in.

Riser height: 7 in.

Tread depth: 10½ in.

Total rise, finished floor to finished floor: 8 ft., 2 in.

LAYING OUT THE STRINGER

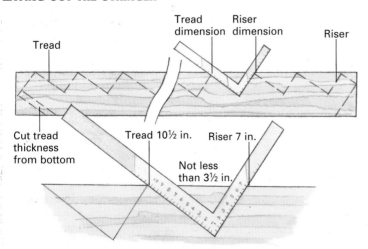

Tread

Tread dimension

Riser dimension

Riser

Cut tread thickness from bottom

Tread 10½ in.

Riser 7 in.

Not less than 3½ in.

CODES FOR STAIRS

WIDTH: (minimums)
■ 36 in. between walls
■ 32 in. between a single handrail and opposite wall
■ 28 in. between handrails on walls

HEADROOM: Minimum 6 ft., 8 in. above any portion of stairway, measured above the tread nosings

TREADS AND RISERS:
■ Minimum tread depth: 10 in.
■ Maximum tread variation: ⅜ in.
■ Maximum tread slope: 2 percent
■ Maximum riser height: 7¾ in.
■ Maximum riser variation: 3/16 in.

TREAD AND RISER PROFILE:
■ Nosing must be ¾ to 1¼ in.
■ No nosing required for treads over 11 in.
■ Risers can be up to 30 degrees from vertical

WINDER STAIRS:
■ Tread must be at least 10 in. at a point measured 12 in. from the narrow side
■ The tread must be at least 6 in. deep
■ A handrail is required on the narrow side

SPIRAL STAIRS:
■ Minimum width for any stair: 26 in.
■ Treads must be at least 7½ in. at a point measured 12 in. from the narrow side
■ Maximum riser height: 7¾ in.
■ Minimum headroom above any portion of a stairway: 6 ft., 6 in.

LAYING OUT THE STRINGER

Stringers have to be strong; cut them from straight 2×12 lumber with few or no knots. Here's how to mark the notches for the cuts that will support the treads and risers:

- Set one stringer on your workbench or across sawhorses and label the right end as the top and the left as the bottom of the stairs. Put tape on the tongue (short leg) of your framing square to mark the riser dimension (7 inches in our example). Mark the blade (long leg) at the tread depth (10½ inches).
- Lay the framing square on the stringer—tongue to the right (or top)—so the marks intersect the top edge of the board, as shown in the illustration on the opposite page. Scribe the angle of the square on the stringer.
- Continue along the stringer until you have marked all the treads and risers.
- Mark the bottom of the bottom riser shorter by the thickness of the tread so the tread height will be the same for all steps. Mark a notch for the lower 2×4 cleat and one at the top for a ledger or joist hanger, then cut out the notches.
- Set the stringer in the opening and make adjustments if necessary. Use this stringer as a template to mark the others.
- Install the bottom cleat and top joist hangers. Then fasten the stringers into place.

FINISHING THE STAIRS

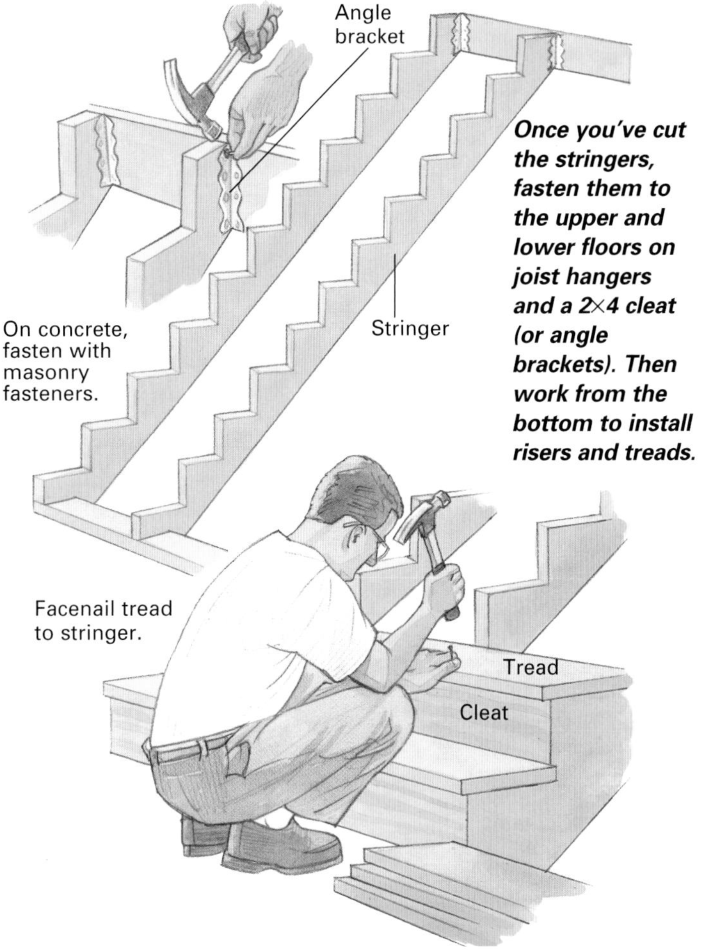
Angle bracket
On concrete, fasten with masonry fasteners.
Stringer
Facenail tread to stringer.
Tread
Cleat

Once you've cut the stringers, fasten them to the upper and lower floors on joist hangers and a 2×4 cleat (or angle brackets). Then work from the bottom to install risers and treads.

TREADS AND RISERS

Cut treads from round-nosed tread stock and risers from either 1× stock or ¾-inch plywood. Fasten two or three risers at a time, then starting at the bottom, attach the treads with construction adhesive and ringshank nails.

Facenail the treads to the stringers and the risers from the back. The combination of construction adhesive and the extra holding power of ringshank nails should keep your new stairs from squeaking.

SAVE YOUR STAIRS

New stairs will take a beating from other construction activities. Cover the treads with heavy paper to protect them. Leave the finish work until the end.

A SAMPLING OF STAIR DIMENSIONS

Total Rise Feet/inches	Number of Steps	Riser Inches	Tread Inches	Total Run, Feet/inches
7 ft./6 in.	12	7½ in.	10 in.	9 ft./2 in.
7 ft./7 in.	13	7 in.	10½ in.	10 ft./6 in.
7 ft./10¼ in.	13	7¼ in.	10¼ in.	10 ft./3 in.
8 ft./½ in.	13	7½ in.	10 in.	10 ft.
8 ft./2 in.	14	7 in.	10½ in.	11 ft./4½ in.
8 ft./3¾ in.	14	7⅛ in.	10⅜ in.	11 ft./2⅞ in.
8 ft./5½ in.	14	7¼ in.	10¼ in.	11 ft./1¼ in.
8 ft./7¼ in.	14	7⅜ in.	10⅛ in.	10 ft./11⅝ in.
8 ft./9 in.	14	7½ in.	10 in.	10 ft./10 in.

SAFE STAIRS

Steep stairs take up less space, but increasing the angle compromises safety. A stairway angled at 38 degrees takes up 30 percent less space than one at a 35-degree angle, but that 3-degree difference represents a big increase in the pitch of the stairs. The ideal stair angle is between 30 and 35 degrees.

WIRING BASICS

TYPICAL NEW FRAME ELECTRICAL ROUGH-IN

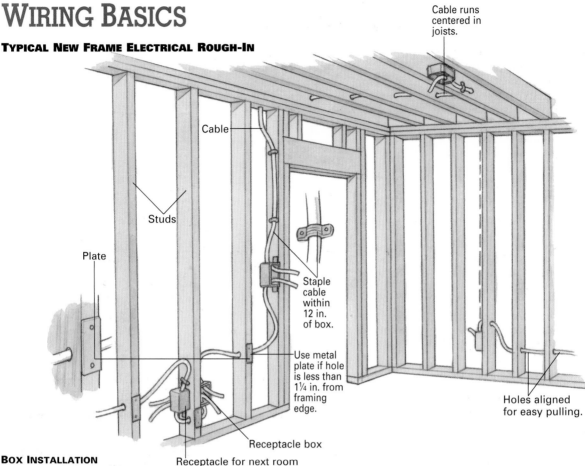

Cable runs centered in joists.

Cable

Studs

Plate

Staple cable within 12 in. of box.

Use metal plate if hole is less than 1¼ in. from framing edge.

Holes aligned for easy pulling.

Receptacle box

Receptacle for next room

BOX INSTALLATION ON BLOCK WALL

Masonry anchor

Surface box

Conduit

Cable

White   Black

Ground wire

Any room conversion requires adding at least one circuit for lighting. Media rooms, workshops, and other rooms may require more. Your wiring plan will show where you want lights and electrical outlets. Getting the wires to those places is easiest when you are working with new, unfinished framing. It's more difficult when you have to get the power through existing walls.

WIRING A NEW FRAME WALL

Nonmetallic cable (sheathed in a tough plastic) or BX cable (with flexible metal sheathing) must be supported in the framing. Here's how:

■ For runs parallel to the framing, staple or clamp it to the widest face of the framing.
■ For runs perpendicular to the framing, drill ¾-inch holes. This is easier if you know where the wires go before assembling the framing. After you cut the framing members to length, clamp them and drill all the holes at once with a spade or auger bit. This makes the holes line up straight. To avoid weakening

the lumber, drill the holes 1¼ inches from the face of vertical framing, 2 inches from the face of horizontal framing. (See "Codes for Cable" on the opposite page.)
■ When running cable through joists, drill near walls, if possible. Protect surface-mounted cable that runs perpendicular to joists in unused attic space with 1× stock laid flat on both sides of the wire.

BOXES AND RECEPTACLES

Electrical boxes come in different styles for different applications. Choose boxes that are large enough for the devices and connections

COPPER WIRE SIZES AND TYPICAL USES

Wire Size	Typical Use
18	Lamp cord, low-voltage circuits
16	Low-voltage circuits
14	Lighting circuits
12	Small appliance/lighting circuits
10	Water heater, clothes dryer

they will hold. Also consider how you will attach the box to your framing, and choose one with the correct mounting style. Pry off the knockout in the hole(s) that will make cable entry easiest. Pull enough wire to connect the receptacle, and tighten the bushing clamp or the clamp at the rear of the box.

Wires in the cable are color-coded, and certain wires go to specific terminals:

BLACK: the hot wire, connects to the brass or darkest terminal of the receptacle or switch.

WHITE: the neutral wire, connects to the silver terminal.

RED: A second hot wire in a 220-volt receptacle.

BARE OR GREEN: the ground wire, connects to the green screw or to the box itself.

CABLING AN EXISTING WALL

Most new circuits will originate from a lower floor through the bottom plate of a wall. The problem is, you can't see the bottom plate. But you can find it by working from the upper stories, using the methods shown in the illustration at upper right. Run new wiring through interior walls only. Exterior walls usually contain insulation and other obstructions. In some cases, you may have to drill more than one hole in walls and ceilings to pull wires for new circuits. For complex installations, call an electrician.

RUNNING A NEW CIRCUIT TO THE ATTIC

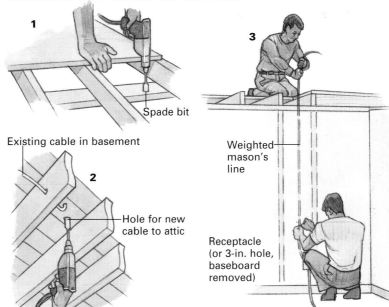

Spade bit

Existing cable in basement

Hole for new cable to attic

Weighted mason's line

Receptacle (or 3-in. hole, baseboard removed)

1. Determine the entry point for new circuit—directly above an existing lower-story wall. Drill a ¾-in. hole through the top plate of attic wall above an existing outlet. (If no outlet exists, remove a baseboard and cut a 3-in. hole at the base of wall, then drill a ¼-in. locator hole into the basement.)

2. Find the circuit in the basement that feeds the outlet and drill up 4 in. to either side of the wire. (Or enlarge the locator hole when no outlet is present.)

3. Drop a weighted mason's line from the hole in the attic and pull it through the outlet hole (or cutout). Feed a fish tape up from the basement and tie it to the mason's line. Attach the cable to the fish tape in basement. Pull the line up with the fish tape and the cable attached.

CODES FOR CABLE

■ Staple or clamp every 54 inches (except BX cable between ceiling fixtures less than 6 feet apart) or through holes 1¼ inches from the face of vertical framing, 2 inches in horizontal framing.
■ Where recessing is impossible, protect with steel plate.
■ Holes in metal framing must be bushed. Holes in boxes must be bushed or cable otherwise protected from chafing.
■ Support cable no more than 12 inches from a box with a clamp, no more than 8 inches from a box without a clamp (for BX cable, 24 inches maximum, where flexibility is required).

CODES FOR RECEPTACLES

CONVENIENCE OUTLETS:
■ Required in every habitable room, on walls wider than 2 feet (including counters and dividers), spaced at 6-foot intervals.

SEPARATE SMALL-APPLIANCE OUTLETS:
■ Required—two 20-amp circuits in kitchen, one in pantry, laundry, dining room.
■ No point on a kitchen counter can be more than 2 feet from an outlet.
■ Faceup receptacles are forbidden.

GFCIS (REQUIRED LOCATIONS):
■ Outdoors, at front and rear of house, if the receptacle is accessible from the ground.
■ Next to lavatory and within 6 feet of the kitchen sink.
■ In a garage or unfinished basement.
■ Near a pool or service to a whirlpool tub.

PLUMBING BASICS

Before you start any plumbing work, you'll need a detailed plumbing plan—both for your own reference and to get approval from your building department. Building code officials can also help you decide on the best location and routing of added plumbing lines.

Local codes vary widely on the material (copper and various

PLUMBING SOLUTIONS

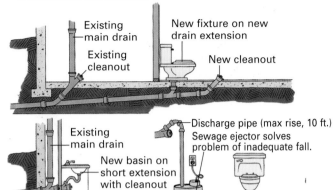

plastics), size, and thickness of pipes allowed in both supply and drain-waste-vent (DWV) systems. Check before you purchase pipe.

ROUGHING IN

Rough in the location of the lines first. Expose the framing in existing walls that will be replumbed and cut holes in its framing. Or cut them in the framing of a new wall. Start with the DWV pipes—maintaining the required fall of ¼ inch per foot—then lay out the supply lines. Space supply lines parallel and 6 to 8 inches apart. Refer to the illustration at left, and follow the guidelines that follow when cutting holes.

JOISTS:
■ Never cut holes in girders or in the middle third of joist length.

■ In the end third of joist length, limit hole size to a sixth of joist depth, elsewhere a third of depth and at least 2 inches from an edge.

TYPICAL PLUMBING ROUGH-IN

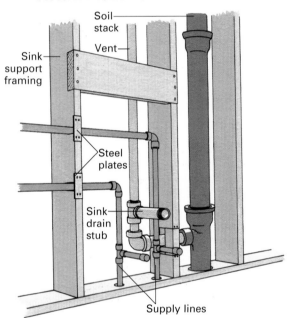

NO-HUB CONNECTOR

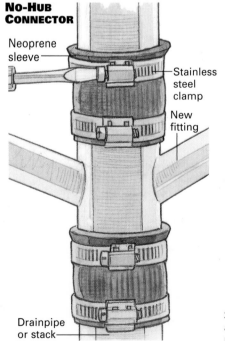

JOINING PLASTIC PIPE

1. Cut pipe with hacksaw or backsaw.

2. Remove burrs with a knife.

3. Mark both sides of joint for proper fit and apply solvent cement to both pieces.

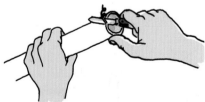

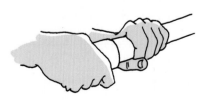

4. Join pieces and quickly rotate until marks are aligned. Hold for 15 seconds.

JOINING COPPER PIPE

1. Cut pipe with tubing cutter. Remove inside burrs.

2. Clean both parts of joint with emery cloth or sandpaper until shiny.

3. Apply flux.

4. Rotate the pieces.

5. Apply flame to fitting and pipe until flux bubbles.

6. Flow solder by touching to joint.

STUDS:

■ Limit hole size to a fourth of stud width in a bearing wall, about three-eighths of width in a nonbearing wall, ⅝ inch from an edge.

JOINING PIPE

Plumbing requires the right connections, and the techniques differ for copper pipe and plastic. Copper connections are generally soldered (or *sweated*), but solder won't hold in a wet pipe, so be sure to drain existing pipes thoroughly. Plastic pipe requires a special solvent cement; it's combustible, so ventilate the area when you're working with it.

Connection of either material requires smooth cuts without burrs. Cut copper with a tubing cutter and plastic with a hacksaw. Follow the directions in the illustrations.

NO-HUB CONNECTORS

A no-hub connector is a clamp consisting of a neoprene sleeve, a stainless steel shell, and two compression bands. No-hub connectors simplify connecting new lines to the main stack or main drain (either cast-iron or plastic pipe). They also join plastic or copper pipe.
■ First, hold the new fitting against the existing pipe and mark the pipe for cuts that will accommodate the fitting and extensions. Cut the existing pipe with a soil-pipe cutter, a circular saw with a metal blade, or a hacksaw.
■ Slide the no-hub onto the existing pipe, pushing the center ridge to the pipe end.
■ Glue pipe extensions to the new fitting and slide them into the no-hub. Then tighten the clamps.

CODES FOR PLUMBING

SUPPLY PIPING:
■ Must be at least ¾-inch pipe.
DWV PIPING:
■ At changes of direction, connect drainpipe through a wye, tee wye, bend, sweep, or sanitary tee or fittings with appropriate sweep. Multiple fittings from two or more branches are allowed if the branches are the same size and are from similar fixture types or groups; exceptions are kitchen sinks and toilets.
TRAPS: Every fixture must have an individual trap except for:
■ Fixtures with integral traps, such as toilets.
■ Multibowl sinks with outlets less than 30 inches apart.
CLEANOUTS: Install a cleanout fitting:
■ In cumulative horizontal runs of 75 feet and at any change of direction greater than 45 degrees, except when direction change is within 40 feet of another.
■ For accessibility, with an 18-inch clearance for 3- and 4-inch pipe, and 12-inch clearance for smaller pipes.
VENT TERMINATION:
■ Must not be under a window or door, within 5 feet horizontally and 2 feet below a door or window, and must extend at least 6 inches above the high side of the roof.

REMODELING YOUR ATTIC

Remodeling your attic will be relatively easy if you know basic construction techniques, have the right tools, and, of course, work from your dimensioned floor plan.

Gather tools and materials in the attic before you start. Having everything on hand saves time and stress; you'll quickly become weary of repeated trips up and down the attic stairs—or ladder, if the stairs aren't built yet.

AVOID CRACK-UPS

An attic renovation can stress the ceiling in the room below. The shock of nailing new joists, subfloor, or the bottom plates of partition walls can spread over the whole surface and cause cracking.

There's no guarantee that a ceiling won't crack, but you can minimize the problem by using a nail gun or screws instead of a hammer and nails.

You can let your creativity soar when remodeling an attic, but even the simplest room requires some demolition and some construction. If you have to cut through the roof or build a dormer, pick the best weather for your work. Always follow sound safety practices.

IN THIS SECTION

Installing Attic Stairs **51**

New Attic Floors and Ceilings **52**

Building a Shed Dormer **54**

Building a Gable Dormer **56**

Building Attic Walls **58**

Installing Attic Windows and Doors **60**

Skylights and Roof Windows **62**

Installing Vents and Insulation **63**

FROM FRAMING TO FINISH

Although your attic remodeling project may have peculiarities that change the normal order of construction, most attic conversions go smoothly if you do the work in this order:

- Installation or modification of stairwell.
- Floor joists strengthened or new joists added.
- Wiring, plumbing, HVAC alterations to floor.
- Install insulation, floor, and roof.
- Install subfloor.
- Roof frame alterations.
- Dormer construction.
- Partition wall and ceiling framing.
- Electrical, plumbing, and HVAC stub-ins to walls and ceilings.
- Wallcoverings and other finish work.

INSTALLING ATTIC STAIRS

Constructing a stairway begins with a hole in the attic floor, one that's already there, or one you cut. Whether you're enlarging existing stairs or building a new stairway, the procedure is the same.

You can orient your stairwell opening either perpendicular to or parallel with the attic floor joists. Parallel construction will require much less cutting.

MARKING AND CUTTING THE OPENING

First, erect temporary supports perpendicular to the attic floor joists and about two feet beyond your proposed stair location.

■ Using your detailed floor plan, lay out the perimeter of the opening on the attic floor or on the floor joists. Snap chalk lines to mark where you will make cuts—at the finished width of your stairwell (see page 44).

■ Set your circular saw to the depth of any existing flooring and cut along the chalk lines. Use a carbide-tipped blade—you may cut through flooring nails.

■ Remove flooring and any insulation. Disconnect plumbing and wiring and reroute.

■ At the corners, drill small holes through the ceiling below. Snap chalk lines between the holes in the ceiling material and cut it away. If you're not removing the entire ceiling, use the techniques for removing wallboard or plaster outlined on page 36.

■ Using a square, extend the perimeter line of the opening down the face of any joists to be cut. Have a helper support these joists or support them with temporary 2×4s while you cut them with a reciprocating saw.

■ Cut trimmer joists and header stock to the dimensions of the opening and nail them with 16d nails staggered at 12-inch intervals.

■ Frame the walls for an enclosed stairwell.

EASY STAIRWAY OPTIONS

Building a stairway is a major undertaking. If you're not sure of your ability with the details but you want to do part of the work yourself, try one of these options:

■ Have a local millwork manufacturer prefabricate and deliver the unit, then install it yourself.

■ Hire a contractor to build the stairs; arrange to help with the installation.

■ Take your stair calculations to a specialty shop and order precut stairway parts that you can assemble.

CUTTING A STAIRWAY OPENING

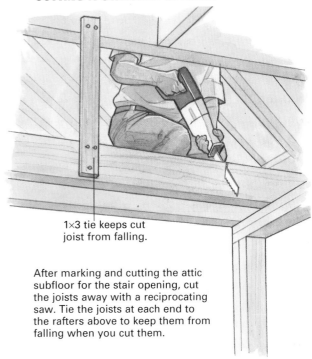

1×3 tie keeps cut joist from falling.

After marking and cutting the attic subfloor for the stair opening, cut the joists away with a reciprocating saw. Tie the joists at each end to the rafters above to keep them from falling when you cut them.

HANGING THE STAIRS

■ Mark and cut the stringer (see page 44), fasten it to the new headers and to the floor below, and install the risers and treads.

■ Don't install the handrail until the final stages of your project. It will be in the way as you move tools and material into the attic during construction.

ROUGH OPENING OPTIONS

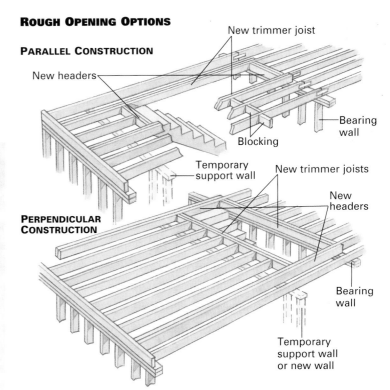

PARALLEL CONSTRUCTION

New trimmer joist

New headers

Bearing wall

Blocking

PERPENDICULAR CONSTRUCTION

Temporary support wall

New trimmer joists

New headers

Bearing wall

Temporary support wall or new wall

NEW ATTIC FLOORS AND CEILINGS

Making changes to attic floors and ceilings involves special techniques. For example, new joists have to span the attic floor completely—from the outer edges of one top plate to the other—or join above bearing walls. In almost all cases, you'll have to angle the top corner of the new joists to fit snugly against the roof sheathing.

Adding new joists means working across the unfinished surface of the old joists. To work comfortably and avoid stepping through the ceiling below, lay temporary catwalks of either 2× stock or loose plywood sheets across the old joists. Once you cut the joist angles, lay the new joists in their locations before you start fastening them to minimize the time spent walking on your temporary flooring.

CUTTING CORNERS

To measure the angle for the joist ends, get as close as you can to the top plate and slide the base of a t-bevel gauge along the top of an existing joist. Adjust the blade of the gauge so it lays against the bottom of the rafter. Tighten the bevel and transfer the angle to a new joist. Repeat for the other end of the joist. Once you determine the correct angle, cut all the joists at the same time.

ADDING NEW JOISTS

You have two options when adding new joists to an attic floor. Which one you choose depends mostly on the size of the existing stock. In either case, if your attic plans include a partition wall, double the joists under the wall and leave a 3½-inch space between them for wiring or plumbing.

Fastening new joists may be difficult—the angle of the rafters at the eaves may not leave you enough room to swing a hammer. Use a nail gun or drive screws.

■ If your existing floor is 2×4 stock, install an independent set of new joists between the old ones. Space the new joists evenly and support them on 2×4 blocks so they clear the existing wiring. A better way is to drill the new stock and rethread the wires.

Toenail the new joists to the cap plates with three 16d nails at each end. If you have

MEASURING JOIST SIZE, SPACING, AND SPAN

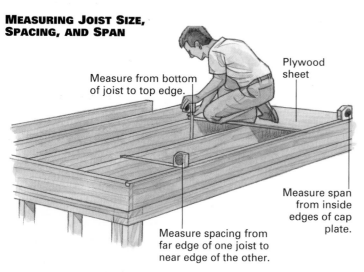

Measure from bottom of joist to top edge.

Plywood sheet

Measure spacing from far edge of one joist to near edge of the other.

Measure span from inside edges of cap plate.

ANGLING THE RAFTERS

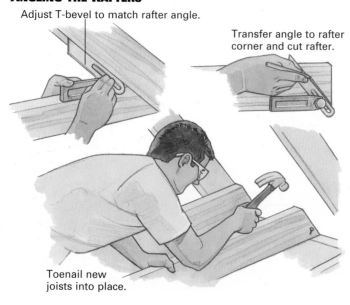

Adjust T-bevel to match rafter angle.

Transfer angle to rafter corner and cut rafter.

Toenail new joists into place.

GETTING JOISTS TO THE ATTIC

If your attic room conversion requires strengthening the floor by adding joists, getting the new joists up to the attic may be your most difficult task. The joist required to span your attic floor may be too long to make the turns up the stairs.

If you're planning a new stairwell, bring the joists up through the opening before you hang the stringers. The rough opening should provide you enough room.

If that won't work, consider stripping away a long section of roofing at the eaves and sliding the joists in from the roof or from scaffolding outside the house. Using outside access will also make it easier to trim the top corners of the joists to fit the rafter angle where the joists butt against the roof sheathing.

to lap them over a long span, center the joint on the cap plate of a lower bearing wall. Either facenail the overlapped sides of the joint or reinforce butt-joined ends with a 2-foot length of ½-inch plywood on each side. Secure the joint with 16d nails and toenail it to the top plate of the supporting wall.

■ If your existing joists are 2×8 or larger, sister a new set to the old ones. Your building codes may also require bridging, usually over bearing walls and every 10 running feet.

Start by clamping the joists together and toenailing the new joists to the cap plates with 16d nails. Leave the clamps in place and stagger 16d nails at 12-inch intervals along the joist. Replace bridging as you go.

LAYING AN ATTIC SUBFLOOR

Using the techniques described on page 34, install plywood subfloor over your floor joists. Begin either along the eaves or on a centerline marked on the joists with chalk. Stagger the joints.

There is no structural need for heavy plywood in areas used only for storage—½-inch material is sufficient for storage weight. Nor is it necessary to lay flooring behind knee walls if the area will not be used. Laying a floor over unused space, however, will keep dust and insulation fibers from migrating into living areas.

INSTALLING CEILING JOISTS

Aside from the nooks and crannies associated with attic construction, finished attics usually have either cathedral or flat ceilings.

CATHEDRAL CEILING: If you plan a cathedral ceiling, your rafters are your framing. You can leave the collar ties in place as long as they're spaced 4 feet on center; raise them one at a time, or—where codes permit—replace them with knee walls.

FLAT CEILING: Unless the collar ties are at the correct height and meet code for the ceiling span, a flat ceiling will require the addition of ceiling joists, usually 2×4s or 2×6s. Use the same procedures for determining the ceiling joist angle

as you would for floor joists and facenail them to the rafters. Drive one 16d nail at one end, level the joist, and fasten the other end. Then finish nailing both ends.

ATTIC CEILING STYLES

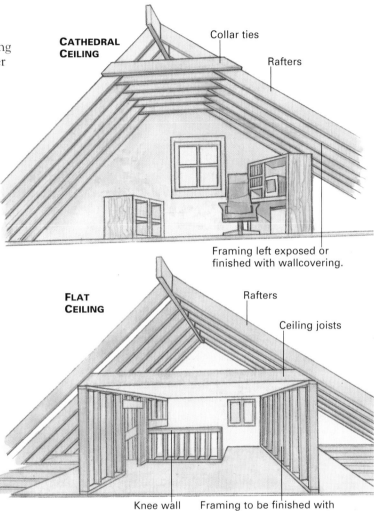

CATHEDRAL CEILING

Collar ties

Rafters

Framing left exposed or finished with wallcovering.

FLAT CEILING

Rafters

Ceiling joists

Knee wall

Framing to be finished with wall and ceiling covering.

LAYING PLYWOOD SUBFLOOR

Offset panel joints

Pick up edge of panel and slide it into place.

BUILDING A SHED DORMER

Building a shed dormer calls for basic carpentry skills and experience with rafters. You can hire a carpenter to cut through the existing roof and frame the dormer for you.

The front wall can either be placed flush with the exterior of the house or set back. A set-back design is more appealing, but it requires the attic floor joists to support the dormer wall. Before you start a set-back dormer, strengthen the floor by adding joists, and lay a subfloor to support the framing.

LAYING OUT THE OPENING

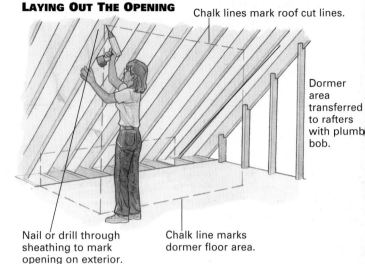

Chalk lines mark roof cut lines.

Dormer area transferred to rafters with plumb bob.

Nail or drill through sheathing to mark opening on exterior.

Chalk line marks dormer floor area.

FINDING THE SLOPE AND DRAWING A PLAN

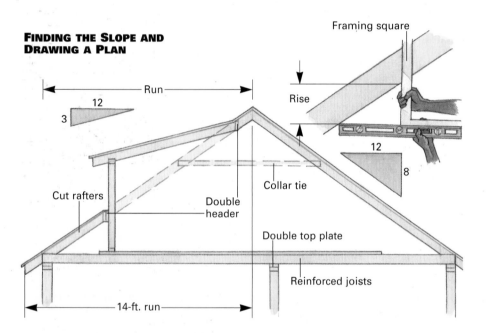

Run

12
3

Framing square

Rise

12
8

Cut rafters

Double header

Collar tie

Double top plate

Reinforced joists

14-ft. run

FINDING THE SLOPE

Draw a section plan for your dormer. Here's what it should include.

MAIN ROOF SLOPE: Slope is the distance a surface rises along a horizontal length. The slope of your main roof is a ratio of its height (attic floor to peak) to the distance from eave to the peak. In the example, the pitch is 8 in 12—the roof rises 8 inches for every horizontal foot.

To determine the slope of your roof without measuring, use a level and a framing square as shown in the illustration above. Where the rafter intersects the square is its rise per foot.

DORMER PLACEMENT: Draw an accurate profile of your dormer and experiment with the placement of the front wall and roof pitch. Aside from the pitch required by code, dormer configuration is largely a matter of aesthetics.

BUILDING THE DORMER

LAYOUT: Snap chalk lines on your attic floor directly below the dormer opening. Drop a plumb bob from the rafters to the corners of the chalk lines and mark the rafters. Reinforce the two rafters at the edges of the opening and drive nails through the roof at the marks.

CUT THE OPENING: Snap chalk lines between the nails on the outside of the roof and strip off the roofing a foot beyond the lines. Snap the lines on the sheathing and with a circular saw set to the depth of the sheathing, cut the sheathing and remove it.

CUT THE RAFTERS: Mark the rafters, and erect temporary walls just beyond the marks (see page 39 for instructions on building a wall in place). Cut the rafters at the marks.

INSTALL DOUBLE HEADERS: Nail double 2×8 joist hangers to the reinforced rafters at the corners of the opening. Slide one header into the hanger and nail it from the opposite side of the rafter. Repeat this process for all the remaining header sections.

FRAME THE FRONT WALL: Remove the temporary walls and frame the front wall with the top plate extended 3½ inches (for corner

CUTTING RAFTERS AND FRAMING
CUTTING THE RAFTERS

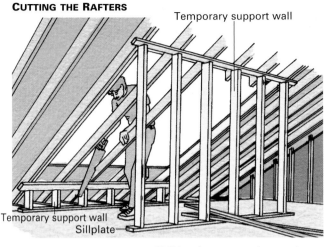

Temporary support wall

Temporary support wall
Sillplate

INSTALLING HEADERS

Nail headers to cut rafters and
facenail header pieces every 12 in.

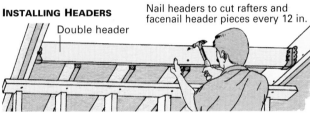

Double header

ERECTING THE FRONT WALL

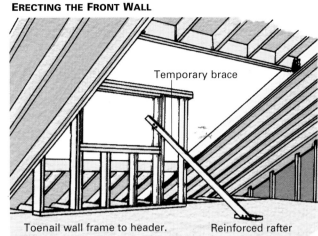

Temporary brace

Toenail wall frame to header.   Reinforced rafter

INSTALLING CORNER POSTS

Facenail end studs to rafters.

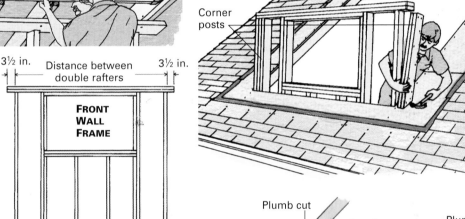

Corner posts

posts) on either
of the end studs.

**SET THE WALL
UP AND BRACE
IT:** Facenail the sill
plate to the floor,
toenail the studs to
the rafter header,
and facenail the end
studs to the rafters.

CORNER POSTS:
Build corner posts
from doubled 2×4s
and ½-inch plywood scraps. Cut
their bottom ends to the angle of
slope of the roof. Facenail the posts
to the end studs and top plate and
toenail them to the rafters under
the sheathing.

CUTTING THE RAFTERS: Set a
framing square on one rafter so the
measurements of the dormer-roof
slope intersect it as shown above.
Mark the plumb cut and the bird's
mouth; test-fit the rafter and make
any adjustments. Use this rafter as
a template to cut the others.

RAFTERS AND ROOFING: Mark
the header and top plate for the
rafters and hang them on the
header with sloping rafter hangers.
Toenail the rafters to the front wall
top plate. Frame and sheathe the
end walls and finish with roofing,
siding, and windows.

3½ in.   Distance between double rafters   3½ in.

FRONT WALL FRAME

INSTALLING DORMER RAFTERS

Plumb cut
Framing square
Plumb cut line
Overhang
Rafter length
Bird's mouth
3 in.
12 in.
Measurements for slope of 3 in 12
Rafters marked on top plate and header.

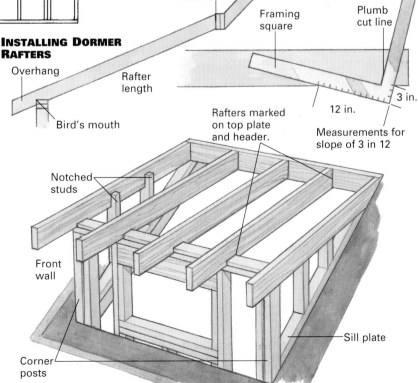

Notched studs
Front wall
Corner posts
Sill plate

BUILDING A GABLE DORMER

A gable dormer is a small room with a peaked roof built perpendicular to the main roof line.

Constructing a gable dormer is slightly more complicated than constructing a shed dormer. The biggest differences are that the top plates of the sidewalls are level and a ridge board supports the roof peak and pairs of rafters on each side. Construction of a gable dormer, however, proceeds in the same order as a shed dormer.

Before you start, strengthen the floor with additional joists and install the proper subfloor to support the dormer framing.

FINDING THE SLOPE

Before you begin construction of a gable dormer, draw a section (or profile) view of it. Using the same techniques discussed for a shed dormer on page 54, find the pitch of your existing roof and draw it to scale on graph paper.

Then draw in the sidewalls to scale and determine the pitch of the dormer roof. The pitch of the dormer roof is the amount of rise in inches (measured from the top plate of the dormer sidewall) for every horizontal foot from the edge of the wall to the centerline of the roof peak. The dormer ridge line is horizontal. In the example, the rise is 6 in 12, but the pitch of your dormer roof will depend on the look of the dormer itself and the pitch of the main roof. Make sketches on tracing paper to get the design right. Then draw the dormer on your final section plan.

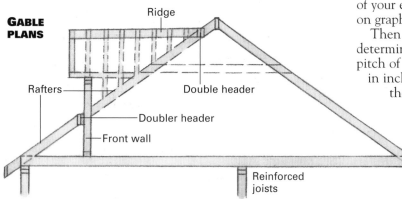

GABLE PLANS

Ridge

Rafters

Double header

Doubler header

Front wall

Reinforced joists

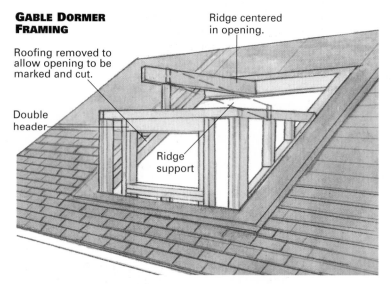

GABLE DORMER FRAMING

Ridge centered in opening.

Roofing removed to allow opening to be marked and cut.

Double header

Ridge support

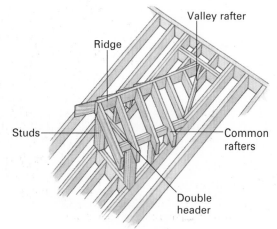

Valley rafter

Ridge

Studs

Common rafters

Double header

CUTTING AND FRAMING

With your section plan as a guide, follow the techniques for building a shed dormer to lay out the gable dormer and cut the opening.
■ Lay out the dormer location on the attic floor and transfer the outline to the rafters with a plumb bob.
■ Mark the roof exterior at the corners and cut the opening through the roof.
■ Build temporary support walls, mark and cut the rafters, and reinforce the rafters at the edge of the opening. Install double headers at the top and bottom of the opening.
■ Frame the front wall as you would a shed dormer and the sidewalls with a doubled top plate as shown, overlapping the front wall cap plates on the sidewalls and extending the top plates of the sidewalls 13½ inches past the front wall. This extension will support the rake rafters.

INSTALLING THE RIDGE

The ridge is supported at the top by the header and at the bottom by a 2×4 ridge stud that is fastened to the front wall top plate.
■ First, cut the ridge to length (the length of the sidewalls, plus the front-wall framing

CUTTING COMPOUND MITERS

The valley rafters and the common and jack rafters that fit against them are cut with compound miters. The angle of the cut conforms to both the downward slope of the boards and the angle where it is attached. To cut a compound miter:

■ Mark the rafter at its longest length—from the end of one angle to the farthest end on the other side.

■ Duplicate the angle of downward slope with an angle gauge and mark it on the rafter.

■ Set your circular saw at a 45-degree bevel and cut along the lines. Go slow—the saw is cutting in two directions and may kick back.

MARKING AND CUTTING RAFTERS

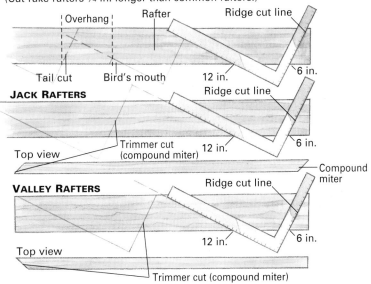

COMMON RAFTERS
(Cut rake rafters ¾ in. longer than common rafters.)

Overhang · Rafter · Ridge cut line · 12 in. · 6 in. · Tail cut · Bird's mouth

JACK RAFTERS

Ridge cut line · 12 in. · 6 in. · Top view · Trimmer cut (compound miter) · Compound miter

VALLEY RAFTERS

Ridge cut line · 12 in. · 6 in. · Top view · Trimmer cut (compound miter)

---

thickness, plus 1 foot for the overhang).

■ Assemble the ridge and ridge stud. The length of the ridge stud equals the rise of the dormer roof minus the width of the ridge board. In the example, it's 18½ inches (24 inches minus 5½ inches—the 2×6 width).

Cut the ridge stud and toenail it 12 inches from the outer end of the ridge board. Lift the assembly into place and fasten the top end to the header in a joist hanger. Toenail the ridge stud to the top plate of the front wall with 10d nails. Level the ridge. Mark the ridge and top plates at 16-inch intervals.

CUTTING THE RAFTERS

There are four kinds of rafters in a gable dormer, and each type requires different cuts. Label them as you cut them.

RAKE RAFTERS: These two are at the front of the dormer and form the overhang.

COMMON RAFTERS: These run from the front wall to the valley.

VALLEY RAFTERS: These run from the intersection of the ridge and header to the sidewalls.

JACK RAFTERS: These short rafters run from the ridge and header to the valley rafters.

■ Lay your framing square on one end of a common rafter with the pitch measurements intersecting at the edge (see illustration on page 54). Mark a line at this point and cut the rafter on the line.

■ Hold the rafter snug against the ridge board and mark the point where the rafter touches the top plate of the sidewall. Lay the framing square at this mark, as shown above, and outline the bird's mouth.

■ At a point 12 inches from the bottom of the bird's mouth, mark a line parallel to the bird's mouth. Cut the rafter on this line and cut out the bird's mouth. Test-fit the rafter, make adjustments as necessary, and use it as a template to cut the remaining rafters.

■ Cut the rake rafters in the same fashion, ¾ inch longer than the common rafters.

■ Measure from the intersection of the ridge and the header to the point where the sidewall meets the main roof rafters. Cut the valley rafters to length and miter the ends.

■ Measure both sets of jack rafters and miter-cut them to length.

■ Toenail all rafters into place with 10d nails. The rake rafters are facenailed to the ridge and toenailed flush with the front of the top plates of the sidewalls.

Sheathe the wall framing and the roof, then finish with roofing and siding, and install the window.

FINISHING THE DORMER

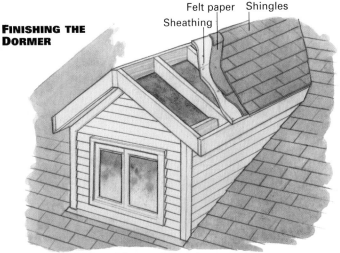

Felt paper · Shingles · Sheathing

Lap siding or siding of your choice

BUILDING ATTIC WALLS

Attic walls may be knee walls, straight partition walls, or sloped partition walls. Many projects include all three types. Build knee walls first, but before you start construction of any wall, strengthen the floor with additional joists as necessary. Construction for each type of wall starts with determining where it will go.

LAYING OUT A WALL

Framing a partition wall is easiest when the wall is directly under rafters or ceiling joists.

If the wall isn't right under rafters or joists, consider repositioning it; moving a few inches either way may not affect your plans. If the wall cannot be moved, install blocking between the rafters or ceiling joists before continuing the layout. Knee walls are built perpendicular to the rafters, so rafter location does not matter for them.

LAYING OUT A WALL

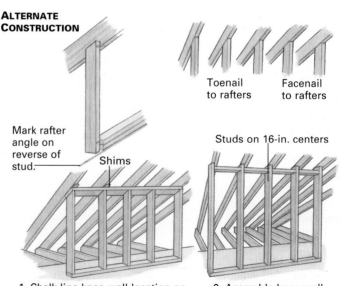

Transfer location of wall to rafters with plumb bob.

Chalk line locates position of wall on subfloor.

of the sill plate position. Snap a chalk line between the marks and adjust the line to make sure the bottom plate lies square to the attic room.

BUILDING KNEE WALLS

These short walls enclose the triangular area at the edge of the roof. Most building codes require knee walls to be at least 4 feet tall. You can build knee walls in place or preassemble them and set them into place, unless sagging rafters or other irregularities make the measurements inconsistent.

Lay out the wall location, then measure the rafter-to-subfloor distance along the wall's length. If the measurements are consistent

Use your attic floor plan to determine where the wall will go. Mark the location of the top plate on the joists or the blocking. Drop a plumb bob to the floor and mark both ends

PARTITION WALL SUPPORT OPTIONS

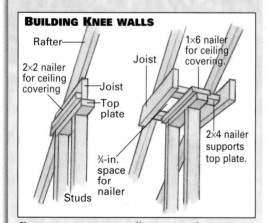

BUILDING KNEE WALLS

Rafter

2×2 nailer for ceiling covering

Joist

Top plate

¾-in. space for nailer

Studs

1×6 nailer for ceiling covering.

2×4 nailer supports top plate.

Framing a partition wall is easier if you locate it directly under rafters or ceiling joists (above, left). Either build the wall in place or install a preassembled wall, fasten it to the joists, and add the nailer to support the ceiling material.

Partition walls between rafters need blocking for support (above, right). Install the joists first, then nail 2×4 blocking between them. Build the wall in place. Start with the 1×6 nailer for the ceiling, then install plates and studs.

ALTERNATE CONSTRUCTION

Toenail to rafters

Facenail to rafters

Mark rafter angle on reverse of stud.

Shims

Studs on 16-in. centers

1. Chalk line knee wall location on floor and rafter. Stack 2×4s on floor to mark studs for cuts.

2. Assemble knee wall, shimming to fit.

within ¼ inch, you can build an assembled wall (see page 39). The knee wall top plate rests on studs cut to the angle of the roof. Scribe the angle on one stud as shown in the illustration on the opposite page, and use this stud as a template to mark the others. Assemble the wall on the attic floor and tilt it into place. Another method is to square-cut the studs to equal lengths, then facenail the bottom plate to them. Stand the wall in place, and facenail the studs to the sides of the rafters. Nail blocking between them.

If the rafter-to-floor distance varies by more than ¼ inch, you may be able to angle-cut the studs and force them into place under the rafters. Severe sagging may require new rafters or a remedy prescribed by an engineer.

BUILDING A STRAIGHT PARTITION WALL

The top plate of a straight partition wall runs flat from one side of the attic to the other. This wall can be erected only in an attic with enough clear space for the necessary 7-foot, 6-inch ceiling height. Constructing a straight wall is a little easier than one with a sloped ceiling. There is no variation in the height of the wall, so you can cut all the studs at once and to the same length.

Once you have marked the location of the wall as outlined above, use the methods shown on pages 38 and 39; either build the wall in place or build an assembled wall.

If you build an assembled wall, you may be able to force its full length into place by pushing the rafters up. It's better to cut the studs ¼ inch shorter than the required length to allow the wall to clear the ceiling or joists and rafters. Shim the difference and nail through the ceiling to the joists.

BUILDING A SLOPING PARTITION WALL

Most attic walls will slope because few attics have enough space for straight walls to the ceiling. You must build sloped walls in place.

Begin by marking the location of the horizontal top plate and the bottom plate as outlined above, either on the rafters or on blocking installed between them. Nail the plates in place. Then cut the sloping top plates to

BUILDING A STRAIGHT PARTITION WALL

Rafter
Ceiling joist
Studs 16 in. OC
Top plate
Door framing
Sill plate fastened to subfloor on chalk line.

1. Mark wall location on floor and rafters.
2. Install ceiling joists.
3. Construct preassembled wall or build wall in place.

length and fasten them also. Using a plumb bob, mark the top and bottom plates for 16-inch stud spacing and measure the length of each stud separately. Cut studs at the angle of the roof and toenail them, checking them for plumb with a level as you go.

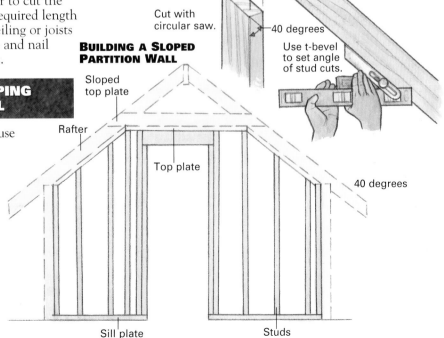

Cut with circular saw.
40 degrees
Use t-bevel to set angle of stud cuts.
BUILDING A SLOPED PARTITION WALL
Sloped top plate
Rafter
Top plate
40 degrees
Sill plate
Studs

INSTALLING ATTIC WINDOWS AND DOORS

REMOVING GABLE-END STUDS

1. Remove top nails with a cat's paw and cut bottom nails with a reciprocating saw.

2. Pry studs away from siding nails with pry bar.

Installing windows and doorways in attics follows the same steps as in other areas in the house. Even though you have to work above ground on gable ends, attic installation is often easier.

PARTITION WALL INSTALLATION

Installation of a window or door in an attic partition wall (or of a doorway in a knee wall) is simply a matter of framing the opening in the wall as you build it in place or preassemble it. Refer to the information in "Door and Window Basics" on pages 40–43, and follow the instructions for attic wall construction on the previous pages. Locate the wall opening where shown by your plan, frame it as you frame the wall, and hang the door or window.

DOORS AND WINDOWS IN GABLE-END WALLS

Rafters and sidewalls support most of the weight of a roof, so gable-end walls are rarely load-bearing. That makes window and door installation easier than on a lower-story load-bearing wall. You don't have to build temporary support walls to cut new openings in nonbearing walls.

Attics often have a window in one or both end walls. Those windows usually provide decorative interest from the outside but little light and ventilation for the inside. Most of these windows are old, single-paned, and poorly constructed. They're probably not right for your new room, but the framing for an old window opening may be suitable for installation of a new window.

If the framing is in good condition and the window is large enough and properly located for your plan, measure the rough opening and order an energy-efficient replacement unit that will fit.

If the existing window is unsuitable or there isn't one, you can move or enlarge an existing opening or cut a new one. The illustrations on these pages show how to make rough openings to install a window. You can use the same techniques to install exterior attic doorways—to a second-story deck, for example—except that the opening is larger and the header construction is different. Follow the procedures outlined here, altering them for doorways as appropriate.

BE WARY OF RIDGE BEAMS

Although gable-end walls are not usually load-bearing, there is one exception: a roof supported by a ridge beam. Ridge beams commonly support cathedral ceilings, transferring the weight normally borne by the sidewalls to the end walls of the structure. These beams are often made of heavy lumber, sometimes glued and laminated.

If you have a cathedral ceiling or an unusually heavy central beam running the length of the house, inspect its construction carefully. It can be modified (as shown by the example at left), but modifying it is expensive and requires professional advice. Consult with a structural engineer before going too far with your plans.

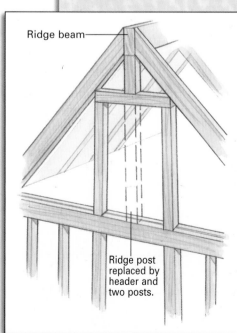

Ridge beam

Ridge post replaced by header and two posts.

FRAMING A GABLE-END OPENING

Frame new opening. At corners, drill holes through sheathing and siding to locate area of siding to be cut.

CUTTING THE OPENING

Nails driven from inside mark corners of opening.

Chalk line

2×4 tacked to siding to guide saw straight.

REMOVING STUDS IN A GABLE-END WALL

Use your floor plan to mark the opening and to determine how many studs you need to remove to make it. Remember, the rough opening for both a door and window is from $\frac{1}{2}$ to 1 inch larger than the new unit. Have the window or door ready to install before you start, or at least order it first, so you're sure of its dimensions. Try to leave an existing stud for a king stud of the new opening. It will save you a little time and lumber.

Pry out the nails at the rafters with a cat's paw and either cut the bottom nails with a reciprocating saw or cut the studs with a handsaw about 4 inches from the bottom plate. Pry the studs away from the siding nails, knock out any remainder, and cut off protruding nails.

FRAMING AND CUTTING THE OPENING

Using the methods shown on page 40, frame the opening by installing the king and jack studs, and the header, sill, and cripples.

Drill holes at the corners of the opening and use the holes as guides to mark the opening on the outside with chalk lines. Working from scaffolding on the outside, cut away the siding on your marks with a reciprocating or circular saw.

INSTALLING THE NEW UNIT

Whether hanging a new door or installing a new window, it's quicker (and safer) to have someone help. Enlist the aid of a helper. Most window units are installed from the outside. Doors can be installed from either side of the opening. Using the instructions on pages 40–43, set the unit in place; center, level, and plumb it; fasten it to the rough opening, and trim it out.

INSTALLING A GABLE-END WINDOW

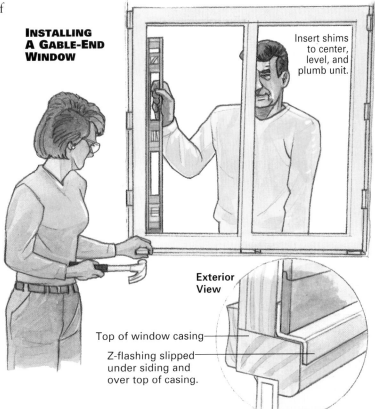

Insert shims to center, level, and plumb unit.

Exterior View

Top of window casing

Z-flashing slipped under siding and over top of casing.

SKYLIGHTS AND ROOF WINDOWS

FRAMING OPTIONS

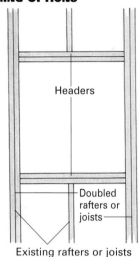

Headers

Doubled rafters or joists

Existing rafters or joists

Although most skylights are designed for do-it-yourself installation, framing the opening requires carpentry skills.

LAY OUT, FRAME, AND CUT THE OPENING

This part of skylight installation is similar to dormer preparation. Referring to the dormer instructions on pages 56–57, mark the opening, install support walls, and cut the rafters. Then frame in the opening, doubling the support members on all sides. Cut the opening and remove only enough shingles for the skylight to rest on the sheathing.

INSTALLING A SELF-FLASHING SKYLIGHT

Test-fit the skylight flange against the sheathing to make sure it lies flat around its entire surface. Coat the edges of the opening with roofing cement and lay the skylight in place with the bottom flange overlapping the shingles. Nail the top and side flanges with roofing nails at 6-inch intervals. Coat the flange entirely with roofing cement and replace the shingles from the bottom up.

INSTALLING A CURBED SKYLIGHT

Build a square 2×4 curb ⅜ inch smaller than the interior of the skylight and toenail the curb to the roof. Flash the curb with step flashing on the sides and with collars on the top and bottom, working from bottom to top so the pieces will overlap to shed rain. Caulk the edge of the curb and set the skylight on it. Drive gasketed aluminum nails through holes in the flange and into the curb.

INSTALLING A SKYLIGHT

SKYLIGHT FRAMING

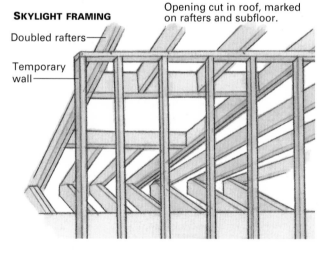

Doubled rafters

Temporary wall

Opening cut in roof, marked on rafters and subfloor.

INSTALLING A SELF-FLASHING UNIT

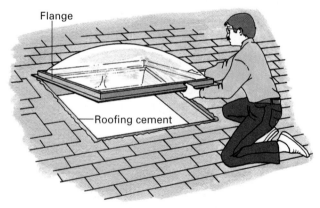

Flange

Roofing cement

INSTALLING A CURBED SKYLIGHT

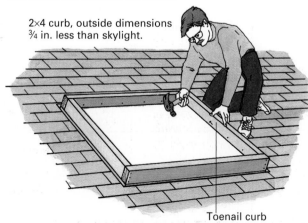

2×4 curb, outside dimensions ¾ in. less than skylight.

Toenail curb

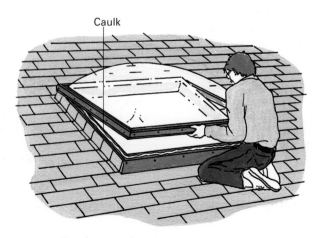

Caulk

INSTALLING VENTS AND INSULATION

You'll need insulation in the roof above your new attic room, but not on the floor below it. Also, if you don't use the space behind knee walls for storage, insulate the knee walls and any floor space behind them. If these area will be storage space, insulate only the roof above them (see illustration at right).

Find out the recommended R-value (a measure of how much a substance resists the transfer of heat) for attic insulation in your area before purchasing the material. Install it before laying the subfloor and building the knee walls.

Venting and insulation go together, not only because they're installed at the same time. Insulation loses its insulating ability when wet; venting lets moisture escape from insulation and helps keep the underside of the roof cooler.

Insulation baffles (sheets of corrugated hard plastic) are available in widths that fit 16- and 24-inch stud spacing. They allow free air passage between the insulation and the roof, and should be used in conjunction with soffit and ridge vents.

INSULATING ATTIC FLOORS

You can insulate attic floors with loose fill, but fiberglass batts and blankets are easier to handle and make much less dust and mess.
■ Begin by making baffles around recessed light fixtures and at the eaves directly above any vents. Toenail 1× baffles about 3 inches from each side of light fixtures to allow heat to escape. Nail baffles along the top plates of sidewalls to keep the batts from covering soffit vents and to allow air to travel upward along the underside of the sheathing.
■ Start a roll of insulation at one edge at the eaves. Unroll it with the vapor barrier side down, pushing it under any existing wiring and cutting it to fit around bridging. Insulate the eaves along one side of the attic, then do the other side. Next, fill in the middle.
■ Where two rolls meet, compress their ends slightly so they fit snugly against each other.

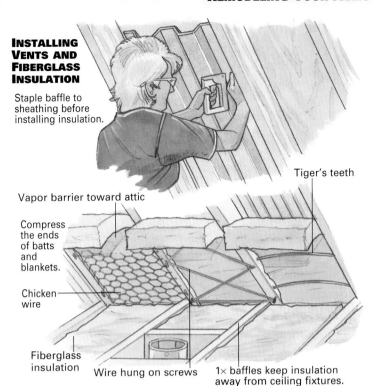

INSTALLING VENTS AND FIBERGLASS INSULATION

Staple baffle to sheathing before installing insulation.

Tiger's teeth

Vapor barrier toward attic

Compress the ends of batts and blankets.

Chicken wire

Fiberglass insulation

Wire hung on screws

1× baffles keep insulation away from ceiling fixtures.

VENTING AND INSULATING THE ROOF

Many older homes do not have rafters deep enough to accommodate the thickness of both insulation baffles and the batts or blankets. If your rafters are too narrow, add 2× furring to them.
■ Working from the bottom of the eaves to the roof peak, staple the insulation baffles between the rafters.
■ Tuck the batt or blanket into the rafter cavity, stapling batts every 6 inches. Hold blankets in place with chicken wire, wire netting, or tiger's teeth as shown in the illustration above.
■ If you install unfaced insulation, cover the entire surface with a 6-mil polyethylene vapor barrier, stapling it to the rafters.

FIBERGLASS SAFETY

Fiberglass is made from thin glass fibers that can be released into the air when insulation is installed. The fibers can be extremely irritating to your lungs, eyes, and skin. Wear a respirator, long-sleeved shirt, long pants, gloves, safety goggles, and a hat when working with fiberglass.

CUTTING FIBERGLASS

Fiberglass batts or blankets are easy to cut. Lay a board along the cutting line and compress the insulation against a piece of plywood beneath. Cut the paper backing and fiberglass with a utility knife.

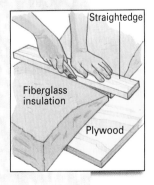

Straightedge

Fiberglass insulation

Plywood

REMODELING YOUR BASEMENT

Remodeling transforms an unfinished basement into comfortable living space. Getting materials like this drywall into the work area may be difficult because of narrow stairs, but the results will be worth the effort.

IN THIS SECTION

Keeping Things Dry **65**

Building Basement Stairs **66**

Preparing a Basement Floor **68**

Building Basement Walls **70**

Installing Basement Doors and Windows **72**

One advantage of remodeling a basement is that the work is probably out of the way of most family activities. If you have a separate basement entry, the project is even less disruptive to normal family routines and more convenient as well.

Although basements are adaptable when it comes to increasing space in your home, there are some obstacles. Plumbing, wiring, and ductwork are often in the way. Supporting walls or jack posts might stand in the middle of your planned family room or office. There may

not be enough light. And the existing stairway might be functional, but not in the style you want for your new living area.

This chapter shows how to apply the basic construction methods described in the previous chapters to the most common needs for a basement makeover. It covers everything from building new walls to tearing out concrete block and installing new windows and doors. Whatever you're planning, however, fix moisture problems first.

KEEPING THINGS DRY

Nothing ruins a remodeled basement faster than moisture. Correct all moisture problems before you begin remodeling. Sealing the wall may solve moderate problems, and installing a sump pump will often cure intermittent water table increases after a sudden downpour. But severe problems may require an interior or exterior drainage system. Consult an engineer or contractor familiar with moisture problems.

SEALING A BASEMENT WALL

Many products are sold as wall sealants; the most effective one is hydraulic cement. Hydraulic cement effectively seals wet surfaces and can stop water flowing through a leak. Hydraulic cement is easy to apply, but the surface must be prepared correctly so the cement will adhere.

CLEAN THE SURFACE: Remove as much of the old paint as you can. Clean it off with a wire brush. Brush away all the loose mortar.

Remove efflorescence (salts that leach to the surface of the wall and appear as white deposits). A stiff brush and a water-soluble etching compound will do the job. The compound can harm you, so wear rubber gloves and eye protection. After cleaning, rinse the wall thoroughly with clear water to remove dust and neutralize the acid. Then let it dry.

PREPARE HOLES AND CRACKS: With a cold chisel, undercut the edges of holes and cracks to make them wider inside than on the surface. This process is called *keying*. Hydraulic cement expands as it cures, and keying ensures the concrete won't pop out. Vacuum the holes and cracks before filling.

PLUG THE HOLES: Use a spray mister to wet the area if it's not wet already. Then force a small amount of hydraulic cement into it with a trowel and smooth it down immediately. If the leak is active, wait until you can feel warmth in the cement—a sign it's beginning to cure. Force the cement into the leak and hold it until it cures. When the patch cures, paint the surface with two coats of waterproofing paint.

INSTALLING A SUMP PUMP

■ Break a hole in the slab. Make it about 6 inches wider and 4 inches deeper than the pump basket. Use a rented jackhammer or a sledge. Put 4 inches of gravel in the hole, insert the basket, and backfill the sides. Trowel concrete level with the basket.

SEALING A BASEMENT WALL

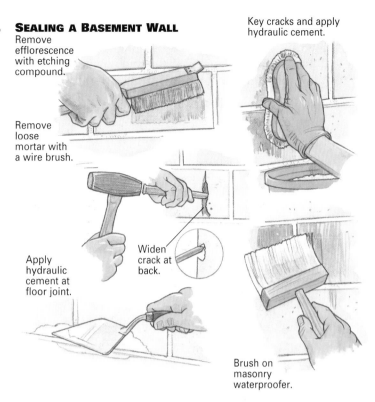

Remove efflorescence with etching compound.

Remove loose mortar with a wire brush.

Apply hydraulic cement at floor joint.

Widen crack at back.

Key cracks and apply hydraulic cement.

Brush on masonry waterproofer.

■ Lower the pump into the basket and connect the drain line to the discharge line. Make electric connections as required (some models simply plug into a nearby outlet).

■ Make a cover if necessary. Drill holes for the pipes and wires through ¾-inch plywood Then saw the board in half—cutting through the center of the holes—to install the cover.

INSTALLING A SUMP PUMP

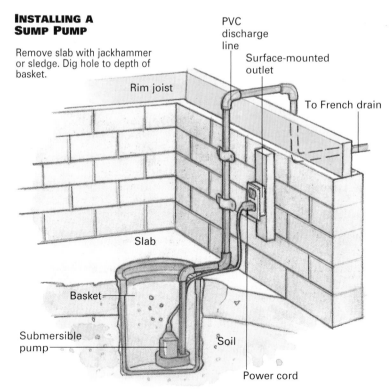

Remove slab with jackhammer or sledge. Dig hole to depth of basket.

PVC discharge line

Surface-mounted outlet

Rim joist

To French drain

Slab

Basket

Submersible pump

Soil

Power cord

BUILDING BASEMENT STAIRS

CUTTING A NEW STAIR OPENING

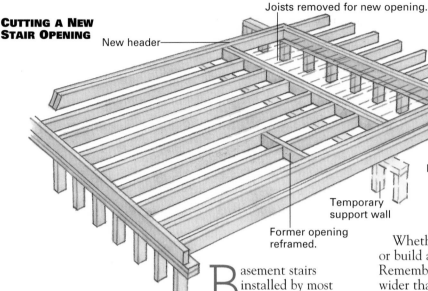

Joists removed for new opening.

New header

Former opening reframed.

Temporary support wall

Bearing wall

Basement stairs installed by most home builders are often steep and narrow, usually built to satisfy minimum code requirements. For an entrance into your remodeled basement, you'll want a stairway that's attractive, safe, and convenient.

An existing basement stairway will probably have to be altered, and that's not always easy. Changing the pitch of the stairs may not be a problem if there's additional room at the bottom.

Enlarging the width, however, can be a major undertaking. Making a stairway wider is only slightly less complicated than cutting a new opening and building a new staircase. After you build a new stairway, fill in and cover the old stair opening, unless you want to have two sets of stairs to the basement.

Whether you alter an existing stairway or build a new one, follow the steps below. Remember that the rough opening must be wider than the finished opening by the thickness of your wallcovering—usually ½ to ¾ inch for each side.

CUTTING OR ENLARGING THE OPENING

Erect temporary support walls even if you're only enlarging the opening. Refer to the illustration at left and on page 51.

■ Reroute any plumbing lines (call a plumber for gas pipes), electrical wires, or ducts that run through the new opening. You may have to remove a finished ceiling to check for—and move—utilities.

■ Lay out and mark the perimeter of the opening on the floor surface above. Strip off any carpeting or tile (you can easily cut through most other types of flooring), then snap new cutting lines if necessary, and cut through the floor and subfloor with a circular saw. Set the saw depth to cut through the

PLATFORM STAIRS: FRAMING THE LANDING

PLATFORM

2×6   Joists   Rim joist

Joist hanger

Plot stair location on basement floor. Then build the platform and platform frame.

FRAME

Top plate

2×4s

Studs   Sill plate

STAIR CHARTS AND TABLES

The hardest part of stair building may be the math. Construction reference tables will give you the answers so you won't have to do the math. Look for books containing stair tables at your local library or bookstore.

The tables list tread and riser dimensions for any total rise and run. And while you're browsing through books, you may also find some of the many manuals on stair design for professionals. These books contain specifications for many stairway designs.

flooring, but not into the joists.
■ Remove the flooring. If there is a finished ceiling below, drill holes at the corners of the opening, then connect the holes to mark the cutout on the ceiling. Remove the ceiling material within the marked area.
■ Working from above or below, extend the cutting lines down the joists. Cut the joists with a reciprocating saw.
■ Measure and cut both the trimmer and header stock and fasten them with 16d nails staggered at 12-inch intervals.
■ Cut stringers, treads, and risers, then hang the stairs in the opening, using the methods outlined on pages 44 and 45.
■ Frame in the old opening by installing new joists in joist hangers. Then install the new subfloor and finished flooring.

BUILDING PLATFORM STAIRS

Platform stairs—two short runs perpendicular to each other— are useful in a tight space where you don't have enough room for a single straight-run stairway.

Check your local building codes, however. Some codes don't allow platform stairs. Others allow them, but set requirements for pitch, width, and other construction details.

Make sure both runs of the platform stairs meet code. Pay particular attention to the pitch. Keep the angle of both runs between 30 and 35 degrees.
■ Lay out and cut or enlarge the opening if necessary, as described above.
■ Frame the end wall at the bottom of the landing if required by your design or your local codes.
■ Measure and cut platform framing members and assemble the platform by facenailing through end joists or by hanging them in joist hangers.
■ Measure and cut studs and plates for platform support walls. Anchor the sill plates in the slab with concrete nails or powder-actuated fasteners. Assemble the support walls in place.
■ Toenail the platform support to the support walls and facenail it to the end and sidewall

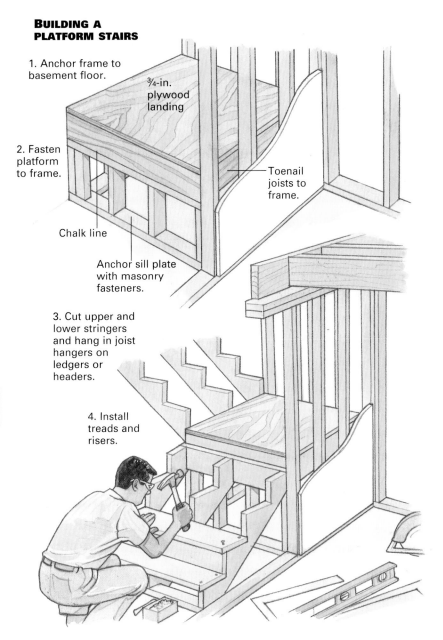

BUILDING A PLATFORM STAIRS

1. Anchor frame to basement floor.

¾-in. plywood landing

2. Fasten platform to frame.

Toenail joists to frame.

Chalk line

Anchor sill plate with masonry fasteners.

3. Cut upper and lower stringers and hang in joist hangers on ledgers or headers.

4. Install treads and risers.

framing if there is any.
■ Nail the lower ledger to the platform support.
■ Referring to the instructions and illustrations on pages 44–45, compute the rise and run of the lower stairs and cut stringers, treads, and risers. Assemble the lower run, cut and install the ¾-inch plywood landing, and repeat to build the upper run.

YOU'LL SWEEP THEM OFF THEIR FEET

If you plan to hang a door at the top of your basement stairs, be sure to include a landing for the doorway. An open stairway door cannot extend over the first step because opening it could knock someone down the stairs. Most local codes require such a landing.

PREPARING A BASEMENT FLOOR

Basement floors need to be dry, level, and free from major defects before you install the finished floor. But you don't always have to remove the existing flooring before laying new flooring.

Some flooring materials can be laid directly on a dry, level, undamaged slab. Others can be laid over an existing finished floor surface. Still others require a new wood subfloor.

If you have carpet on your existing basement floor, and you plan to change the floor covering, the old carpet will have to come up.

QUICK GUIDE TO SLAB-FLOOR PREPARATION

SOLID WOOD STRIP AND PLANK: Not recommended for basements.
SOLID WOOD PARQUET: Lay directly on a slab, on dewaxed resilient flooring if well-bonded to the slab, or on wood subfloor.
MANUFACTURED WOOD FLOORING: Same as parquet.
RESILIENT SHEETS AND TILE: Remove cushioned material and lay new resilient directly on slab or wood subfloor. Smooth well-bonded embossed floors with liquid leveler before laying new flooring.

INSTALLING A BASEMENT BRANCH DRAIN

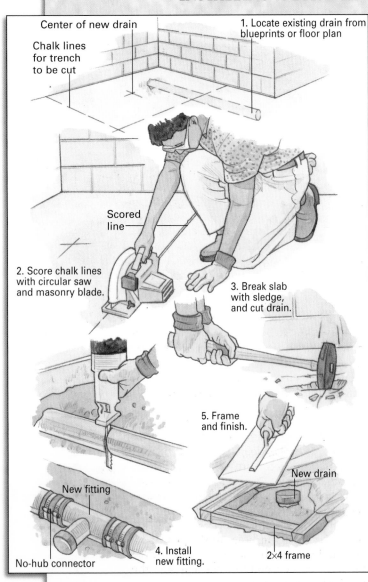

Center of new drain

Chalk lines for trench to be cut

1. Locate existing drain from blueprints or floor plan

Scored line

2. Score chalk lines with circular saw and masonry blade.

3. Break slab with sledge, and cut drain.

5. Frame and finish.

New drain

New fitting

No-hub connector

4. Install new fitting.

2×4 frame

If you want a new bathroom in the basement and you can't piggy-back the new drain lines to the old ones, you may have to tie into them with a branch line. This means breaking up the concrete and installing new lines and fittings. There's some heavy work, but it's not difficult.

Before you tear into the floor, make sure you know exactly where the existing line runs.

■ Mark the position of the existing drain and the branch line on the floor with a chalk line. Have the new shower and toilet on hand before you map your drain lines; plumbing locations need to be precise.

■ Score the lines with a masonry blade in your circular saw. Then break up the concrete between the lines with a sledge. After you get the first chunk out, dig out dirt as far as you can under the remaining sections—concrete is easier to break if there's no soil beneath it.

■ If you aren't sure of the nominal size of the existing line, measure it so you will know what size fittings to buy. Mark the position of the new fitting carefully on the old line. Cut the line with a chain cutter, reciprocating saw, or hacksaw.

■ Install the fitting with no-hub fittings on either side of the cut line. Adjust the fitting with a torpedo level to ensure the correct fall, then tighten the no-hub clamps.

■ Install the new drain line.

■ Recheck the fall of the line over its length, adjust it at either end if necessary, and pour and finish new concrete in the excavated area.

COLORING CONCRETE

You can have a distinctive basement floor—even if your budget won't allow new floor covering or the room you're converting doesn't require it—by adding color to the concrete.

■ Surface dye applies like paint and penetrates the concrete pores. Dye may wear a little longer than paint, but it will have to be reapplied after a while.

■ Good-quality acrylic latex paint can last a surprisingly long time on a properly prepared floor. Etch the floor first with muriatic acid (protect yourself and follow the directions), then clean it with trisodium phosphate (TSP). Scuff a smooth concrete surface with medium-grit sandpaper.

■ Integral dyes are added to the concrete when it is poured. This is a good choice if you're pouring a new slab or covering an old one. Some dyes are sprinkled on the surface of wet concrete. Properly tooled, they can make your floor look like granite or marble.

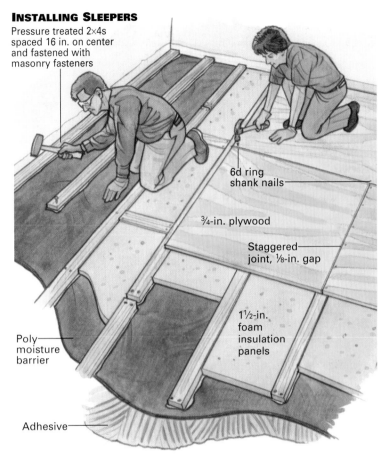

INSTALLING SLEEPERS
Pressure treated 2×4s spaced 16 in. on center and fastened with masonry fasteners

6d ring shank nails

¾-in. plywood

Staggered joint, ⅛-in. gap

1½-in. foam insulation panels

Poly moisture barrier

Adhesive

LAMINATES: Prepare as for resilients.
CERAMIC TILE: Lay tile directly on slab or existing tile, leveled with liquid leveler.
CARPET: Lay conventional carpet directly on slab, well-bonded and leveled resilients, or leveled ceramic tile. Cushioned-backed carpet requires an absolutely smooth surface. If surface is not smooth, install a wood subfloor and lauan plywood.

INSTALLING A WOOD SUBFLOOR

A wood floor with sleepers can solve a variety of basement flooring problems. You can use it when the concrete gets damp from condensation or as an alternative to a liquid leveler when you don't want to fix cracks, tilts, or imperfections. You can install sleepers if you want to insulate the floor. Of course, you must install a wood subfloor if your finished floor will be a nail-down material.

Although a wood subfloor will cover minor cracks and imperfections, its installation begins with a thorough cleaning of the concrete floor. Vacuum the floor, then clean it with a detergent solution and heavy garage brush. Rinse it, and let it dry.

■ Seal the surface with an asphalt primer. When the primer has cured, trowel the slab with asphalt mastic to a depth of about ⅛ inch. Don't trowel yourself into a corner; work toward the doorway.

■ Starting at the door, unroll 15-pound felt paper or 6-mil polyethylene sheets on the mastic, pressing them into the surface to remove air bubbles and overlapping successive sheets by 6 inches.

■ Snap chalk lines on the moisture barrier at 16-inch intervals. Leaving a ½-inch gap at the walls and at the ends of the sleepers, center pressure-treated 2×4s on the chalk lines. Stretch a mason's line tightly across the surface to make sure the sleepers are level and shim the ones that are not.

■ Fasten the sleepers to the concrete with 8d concrete nails, powder-actuated fasteners, or hardened screws. To use the screws, drill a pilot hole through the sleeper to mark the moisture barrier. Lay the sleeper aside and drill the concrete with a masonry bit and hammer drill. Install the screws in the sleepers with a power screwdriver.

■ If you want to insulate the subfloor, cut blocks of 1½-inch polystyrene insulation to fit between the sleepers.

■ Lay a bead of construction adhesive on top of the sleepers, and nail ⅝- or ¾-inch underlayment-rated plywood over them, staggering the joints and leaving ⅛-inch gaps between them, ½-inch gaps at the walls.

■ At the walls, cut holes in the plywood perpendicular to the sleepers. Size the holes for floor registers and install them after the finished flooring is in.

BUILDING BASEMENT WALLS

BASEMENT WALL LAYOUT

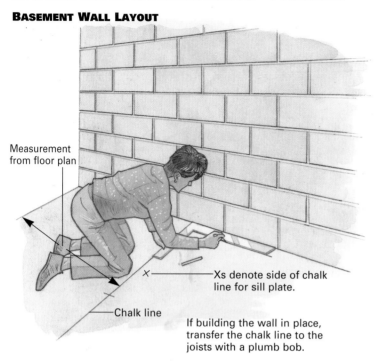

Measurement from floor plan

x — Xs denote side of chalk line for sill plate.

Chalk line

If building the wall in place, transfer the chalk line to the joists with a plumb bob.

METAL FRAMING

Metal studs are often used in home construction. Made of lightweight galvanized steel, they are easy to handle, won't burn, and are not likely to rust. Metal studs are ideal for building nonbearing partition walls. Metal framing is best for building in place, not preassembly.

Metal studs are still called studs, but the top and bottom members are called tracks, not plates.

To build a wall, attach the top track to the joists and the bottom track to the floor. Attach the studs to the tracks with no. 8 self-drilling screws, one at the top and one at the bottom. Cut the track and studs with a carbide-tipped circular saw blade or aviation snips. Install drywall with no. 6 or no. 8 sharp-pointed screws, not drywall fasteners.

Studs have holes punched every 2 feet for wires and pipes. Put grommets in the holes before running the wire or pipe.

When you install a wall in a basement space, you will probably have to cope with mechanical and electrical systems and structural supports.

Basements in older homes, for example, are often divided into small spaces by load-bearing walls. The mortar in these walls often shows the effects of age. Steel beams and jack posts often support the floor above a newer basement, which opens up larger spaces. But the posts themselves may seem to be impediments to building a new wall. Ceiling ducts and pipes may look like problems, too. There are ways to build walls in almost any situation, however.

BUILDING AN INTERIOR WALL

Building a basement wall generally follows the steps outlined on pages 38 and 39. Follow the steps below to build interior load-bearing walls that will accommodate obstructions.

■ First, make sure you have corrected any problems in the slab. The floor must be leveled before erecting walls.

■ Lay out the location of the wall on the floor, keeping it square to the room. Snap a chalk line on the floor to show the position of the soleplate.

■ Erect the wall on the marks. If you're building a load-bearing wall, you'll have to build it in place. Its height has to be exact; you don't want shims holding up the weight of the house. Construct temporary support walls before removing the old support.

■ In most cases, you can build even a load-bearing replacement wall from 2×4 stock, but local codes may specify larger lumber. You also may want to use 2×6 stock if the wall will enclose a jack post.

BUILDING A BASEMENT PARTITION WALL

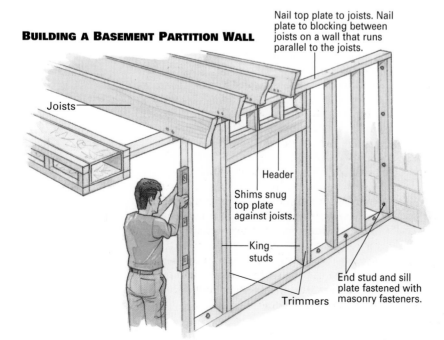

Nail top plate to joists. Nail plate to blocking between joists on a wall that runs parallel to the joists.

Joists

Header

Shims snug top plate against joists.

King studs

Trimmers

End stud and sill plate fastened with masonry fasteners.

PUTTING FURRING ON A BASEMENT WALL

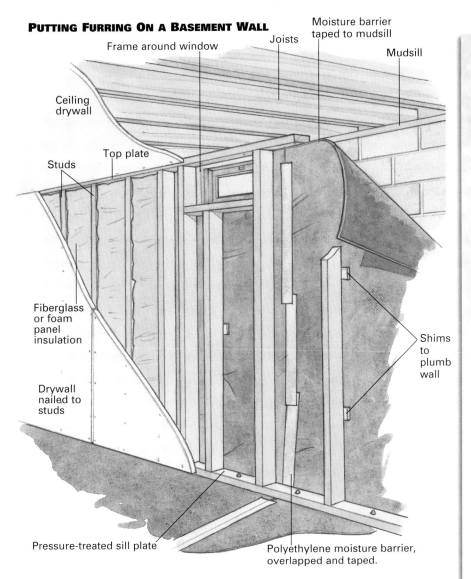

- Frame around window
- Joists
- Moisture barrier taped to mudsill
- Mudsill
- Ceiling drywall
- Top plate
- Studs
- Fiberglass or foam panel insulation
- Drywall nailed to studs
- Pressure-treated sill plate
- Polyethylene moisture barrier, overlapped and taped.
- Shims to plumb wall

POWDER-ACTUATED NAILER

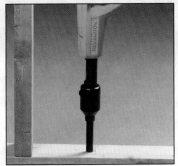

A powder-actuated nailer can make a construction site sound like a shooting gallery. It also makes driving nails into concrete faster and easier—and with less chipping of the concrete.

You can buy one at most home centers or rent one from rental outlets. It's handy for anchoring wood or metal framing to masonry. An explosive charge drives the nail into the material with ease—and with some noise too. Concrete nails (which break or bend if not hit squarely) and hardened screws (which can seem to take forever to install) are slower and less secure than powder-driven nails.

Wear ear and eye protection when using a powder-actuated nailer. Plant the nailer against the surface before pulling the trigger or striking the firing pin.

■ If the wall won't have to bear a load, you can preassemble it. Cut the studs short by ¼ inch so it will clear the joists. Don't expect a full-height wall to clear the basement ceiling joists. You can't lift the weight of the upper stories to make room for a full-sized wall. Shim the gap at the top.

■ With either method, frame any openings as you go, and if possible, predrill the studs and plates for wiring or plumbing runs before the wall goes up.

■ Use pressure-treated lumber for the bottom plate and fasten it to the floor with construction adhesive and concrete or powder-actuated nails. Cut this plate at door openings after the wall is fastened.

■ When you meet a perpendicular obstruction such as ductwork, cut the top plate and frame around the obstruction so you have a surface into which to nail the drywall.

EXTERIOR-WALL TREATMENTS

Furring—2× lumber attached to the surface of a wall—provides a surface to hang the finished wallcovering on and makes space for insulation, wiring, and plumbing.

Start by checking the wall for plumb with a tight mason's line. Mark depressions and shim them when nailing the furring strips. Put up a 2×4 stud wall if the wall is far from plumb. Then staple a moisture barrier to the mudsill and cut the sheets long enough to lap the floor slightly.

Run 2×3s from top to bottom without plates. Fasten the strips to the wall with concrete nails set in the mortar joints, not in the block. Insulate with foam sheets.

A stud wall requires just as much construction time as adding furring to a wall, and the additional depth provides more room for insulation and electrical and plumbing work. Use the wall-construction techniques described in the previous section and refer to the illustration above to install a stud wall on an exterior basement wall.

INSTALLING BASEMENT DOORS AND WINDOWS

Installing a new window or door in an exterior basement wall is a major project. A header or lintel has to be installed in the opening to bear the weight of the house structure and transfer it to the wall, not the window or door.

If you plan to do this project on your own, first consult with a structural engineer, architect, or building contractor.

Cutting reinforced concrete is not a job for a do-it-yourselfer. Hire a professional firm that specializes in concrete sawing. You can cut through a block wall with a rented roto hammer and cold chisels.

To install a below-grade door or a window with a sill that will fall below grade, you'll have to excavate for a window well to keep soil and rainfall away from its exterior surface. You'll probably do much of the excavating in connection with breaching the wall. An above-grade door won't require a well, but you should clear soil at least 6 inches away from the bottom sill.

DIGGING A BASIC WELL

Break through and remove the sod around the location of the new unit. Use the sod to fill in bare spots in the lawn and keep the soil for backfilling the well liner. You can add unused soil to the garden when you're done.

Excavate to a depth that will accommodate whatever drainage system you will use. The depth will be about 2 feet lower than the sill for an independent drain line that runs to a french drain or daylights (opens) at a lower section of your property. Dig to the foundation if you will tie the well drain to an existing perimeter system on the exterior. To construct a light well for your window or a small patio outside a below-grade doorway, excavate to dimensions that will accommodate your design (see page 74). Consider hiring a backhoe operator to dig your drain-line trench if it runs deep and across a large expanse of lawn.

LOWERING THE SILL

When you want to let more light into the basement but you're in doubt about tearing into your foundation wall to build or enlarge a window opening, consider lowering the sill instead of widening the opening.

Lowering the sill allows you to keep the header in place and doesn't always require construction of temporary support walls. (You may want to put one up for safety's sake, though.)

When lowering a basement windowsill, remove the existing window and use the techniques described on these pages to remove just the portion of the wall that will allow installation of the taller window. Don't remove any portion of the wall beyond the sides of the old opening.

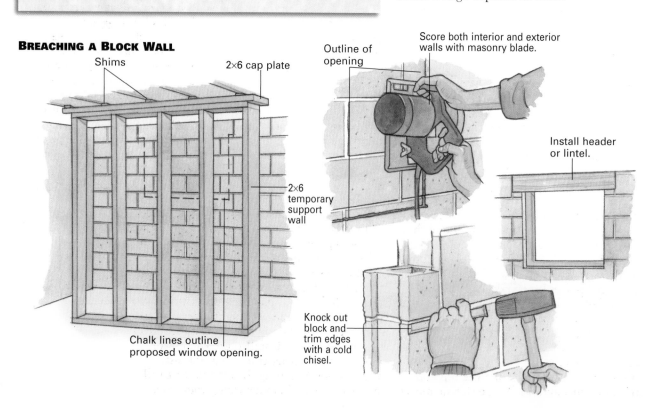

BREACHING A BLOCK WALL

Shims

2×6 cap plate

2×6 temporary support wall

Chalk lines outline proposed window opening.

Outline of opening

Score both interior and exterior walls with masonry blade.

Install header or lintel.

Knock out block and trim edges with a cold chisel.

You don't need to be exact with the excavation for the well itself. You'll need plenty of elbowroom when you cut and frame the opening, and you can backfill it later.

BREACHING THE WALL

First, erect a 2×6 temporary support wall about 4 feet from the exterior wall. Then remove any existing windows.

As with any remodeling task, the location of the new window or door should be shown on a detailed section drawing. Use this section view to locate the exact perimeter of the opening.

Mark the cutting lines on the interior and exterior surface of the wall, and make sure the opening is large enough to accommodate the wood framing and that the rough opening for the unit itself will be on the inside of that framing.

The breach in the wall will be 3 inches wider (the thickness of the 2× framing on both sides) and substantially higher than the rough opening specified for the unit by its manufacturer. Check this specification several times before marking the cut lines.

Using a circular saw with a masonry blade, score the cut lines in several passes—about ¼ inch deeper at a time—on both sides of the wall. Then score another line down the vertical center of the opening so the blocks can be removed easily.

Working from the inside and starting at the center line you scored, tap out the block with a small sledge and finish the edges as flush as you can with a hammer and cold chisel.

FRAMING AND INSTALLING

Use pressure-treated lumber for all framing members on an exterior wall. The size of the framing—window bucks for a window and king and jack studs for a door—will depend on the thickness of the unit. Header stock will be sized not only according to the unit dimensions but also for the amount of weight the header will carry. Measure and cut the header stock (2×10s, 2×12s, a steel plate, or whatever your local code requires) and assemble the pieces.

Install the header first, then the top and bottom framing, and finally the side members

FRAMING THE OPENING

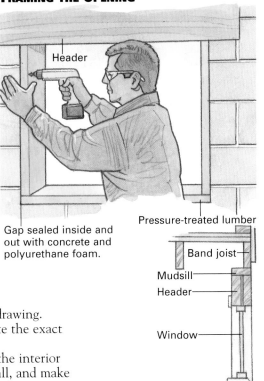

Header

Gap sealed inside and out with concrete and polyurethane foam.

Pressure-treated lumber

Band joist
Mudsill
Header

Window

Sill slanted to shed rain

Block wall

INSTALLING THE WINDOW

Caulk edges of casing.

Casing fastened to window bucks with deck screws.

or king and jack studs. Fasten the framing to the block with galvanized deck screws (if the block will hold the screws), toggle bolts, or other masonry fasteners. Be sure the bottom buck or doorsill tilts slightly to the outside or has a preformed beveled edge to shed rainwater. Seal the gaps between the framing and the block with concrete. When the concrete has cured, fill any remaining gaps around the outside and inside edges with polyurethane insulation. Then fasten the window casing to the bucks with galvanized deck screws and install cladding if the window has aluminum-clad casings. Install the unit using the techniques discussed on pages 40–43 and in the illustration above.

Once you have installed the window or door, you can either trim it out or finish the exterior. Finishing the exterior first will prevent erosion from damaging your work.

EXCAVATE FOR LIGHT

Simply enlarging the well around an existing window is an easy and economical way to increase the light in a basement. Remove the old steel window-well wall, and build a 4- to 6-foot terraced or walled-in light well. You can line the enlarged well with a retaining wall made of rock, poured concrete, or blocks, but terracing is easier and more attractive. The instructions on page 74 can be a basis for your design. Then be creative and add details or materials on the outside to dress it up. Anything you do to create an attractive exterior will improve the view from the interior as well.

INSTALLING BASEMENT DOORS AND WINDOWS
continued

**CREATING A
BELOW-GRADE
ENTRANCE**

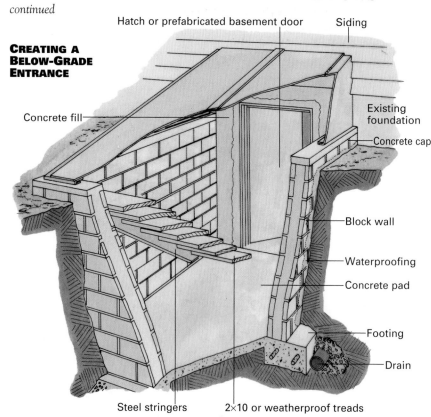

Hatch or prefabricated basement door   Siding

Concrete fill

Existing
foundation

Concrete cap

Block wall

Waterproofing

Concrete pad

Footing

Drain

Steel stringers   2×10 or weatherproof treads

INSTALLING A WINDOW-WELL LINER

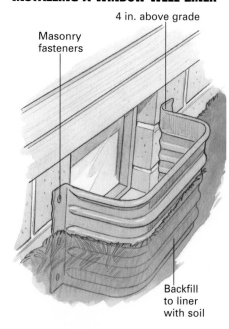

4 in. above grade

Masonry
fasteners

Backfill
to liner
with soil

INSTALLING A WINDOW-WELL LINER

Prefabricated steel liners are not heavy, but positioning and attaching them will require a helper. Before installing the liner, however, complete the excavation and installation of any drain lines.

■ Hold the liner in place against the outside wall so its top edge sits 4 to 6 inches above the soil line.

■ Mark the wall for the position of the fasteners. Drill holes for masonry anchors and fasten the liner to the wall with them.

■ Fill the bottom of the well with gravel level with the drain cover, then backfill the liner with soil, tamping it as you go.

■ Install a ladder if your local codes require one. Most local codes will require a ladder for window wells deeper than 44 inches.

CREATING A BELOW-GRADE ENTRANCE

A below-grade entrance can enhance any basement and will provide years of added convenience. Before you start, order prefabricated steel stringers and steps made for outdoor use.

■ **BUILDING THE AREAWAY:**
Excavate an area large enough for the retaining walls and stairs. Dig the bottom 4 inches below the bottom of the foundation. Build the areaway as large as you can.

Excavate trenches for footings for the walls to dimensions required by your local code.

Set horizontal lengths of rebar in the trench and pour the footings. Then push vertical rebar into the wet concrete every 24 inches and let it cure.

Install a perimeter drain around the areaway and tie it into the existing drainage system or direct runoff to a lower area of your yard.

Starting at the corners, enclose the areaway with block retaining walls to a height even with or slightly above grade.

Waterproof the exterior of the walls with asphalt emulsion or other method required by code.

INSTALLING THE DOOR:. Use the techniques outlined on pages 72–73 to breach the wall and install the doorway.

BUILDING THE STAIRS:. Install steel stringers and steps according to the manufacturer's specifications.

COVERING THE AREAWAY:. Covering the areaway with a hatch door or shelter will give you an all-weather entrance. A prefabricated greenhouse makes an attractive entry and brings in extra light. Either installation requires a poured concrete cap on top of the retaining walls.

TERRACING A LIGHT WELL

You can make the area around basement windows and below-grade doors far more attractive with a terraced light well than with steel liners or concrete retaining walls. Follow the basic steps that follow, and add creative details that go with your interior and exterior landscape design.

EXCAVATE THE SOIL: For a light well at a window, dig the soil back at an angle of no more than 45 degrees and to a depth that will accommodate the drainage system. For a below-grade patio, dig 4 to 6 inches below the doorway and make the excavation wide enough to be comfortable (probably 6 to 8 feet). Then angle the soil line at the top for terracing.

■ Install the drain line in the bottom of the well and cover the floor of the excavation with gravel or poured concrete.

■ Stairstep a series of terraces, using 2× treated lumber, landscape timbers, concrete block, or precast pavers. Plant the terraces with ornamental foliage and decorate them with small architectural accents. You can even install a small self-contained fountain in a medium-sized pot.

TRIMMING BASEMENT WINDOWS

Basement windows present some unique trim challenges. The thickness of basement walls tends to make the windows seem small, and the height of the window might interfere with a suspended ceiling. Tackle these challenges by using the following techniques.

BEVEL THE EDGES: Instead of squaring off the bottom of the window at the walls, slope the edges to reveal more of the window area.

■ Fasten beveled 1× stock along the perimeter of the window frame. Keep the angle between 10 and 30 degrees.

■ Bevel horizontal furring strips or the tops of studs in a stud wall. Fasten 1× blocking between studs to provide a surface for nailing the drywall.

■ Insulate with rigid or fiberglass insulation and finish with drywall.

■ Attach a 1× nailer at the top of the window frame and angle the edge

panels of a suspended ceiling up from the ceiling hangers to the nailer.

STEP THE FRAMING: Instead of beveled stock, use 1×s to build steps out from the window frame to the edge of the walls. You can display decorative items on the multiple windowsills.

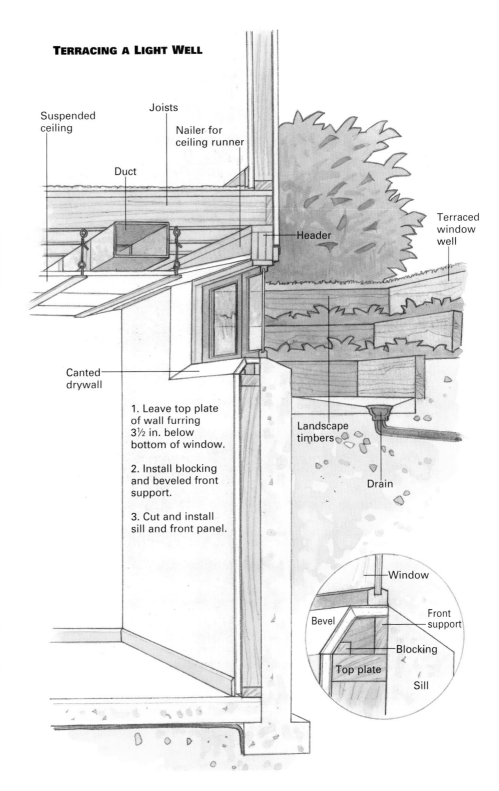

TERRACING A LIGHT WELL

Suspended ceiling

Joists

Nailer for ceiling runner

Duct

Header

Terraced window well

Canted drywall

1. Leave top plate of wall furring 3½ in. below bottom of window.

2. Install blocking and beveled front support.

3. Cut and install sill and front panel.

Landscape timbers

Drain

Window

Front support

Bevel

Blocking

Top plate

Sill

FINISHING TOUCHES

Finishing a room—laying the floor, painting or covering the walls, and installing the woodwork and trim—brings it to life with style, individuality, and personality.

Finish work is exacting. Finishing and trimming require care and patience as well as detailed plans and the proper tools.

You'll find the extra care and craftsmanship worth the effort. Every time you enter the room, you'll take pride in your well-laid floor, the invisible drywall joints, and the tight-fitting molding miters.

IN THIS SECTION

Installing Parquet or Vinyl Tile 78

Installing a Floating Floor 80

Installing Sheet Vinyl 82

Installing Conventional Carpet 84

Installing Drywall 86

Installing Wood Paneling 88

Finishing the Ceiling 90

Closets, Cabinets, and Shelving 92

Trim Work 94

Floor and wallcoverings, ceiling finish, and trim make a room attractive and comfortable. Choose and install the finishing materials carefully.

HOW FLOORING MATERIALS ARE SOLD

Estimating material quantities for your new floor is not the exact science it often seems. All you need to know is how materials are sold and the area of your floor. Then add an extra allowance for doorways, seams, errors, and waste. The information below will get you started.

Flooring Material	Sold By:
Solid-wood strips and planks	Square foot, in bundles. Add 8 to 10 percent. An 8-ft. nested bundle covers 18 sq. ft.
Manufactured flooring	Square foot. Packaging varies by manufacturer.
Tile (parquet, resilient, ceramic, and dimensioned stone)	Square foot, in boxes. Add 8 to 10 percent. The area a box will cover varies with the material and style.
Resilient sheet and carpet	Square yard, in rolls, usually 12 ft. wide. Add 4 in. to each dimension for cutting, 8 to 10 percent for seams, and 20 percent for matching.
Laminates	Square foot, in cartons. Add 8 to 10 percent. The area a carton will cover varies with manufacturer and style.

To estimate quantities for solid-wood flooring, carpeting, manufactured flooring, or sheet flooring, calculate the area of the floor, then add the allowances shown in the chart on the opposite page. Or, take your measurements to the flooring supplier, who will calculate the amount of materials and supplies you need.

TIPS FOR TILE

The best way to estimate tile quantities is to draw your floor to scale on graph paper and draw in tiles so you have a block of full tiles in the center of the room. Erase any tiles on the edges that aren't at least half a tile wide.

ESTIMATING DRYWALL MATERIALS

Wallboard Sheets	Nails, pounds 1¼ in.	1⅝ in.	Screws, pounds 1¼ in.	1⅝ in.	Compound, gallons	Tape, feet
8	1	1½	1	1	2	95
10	1½	2	1	1½	2	118
12	1½	2	1½	1½	3	142
14	2	2½	1½	2	3	166
16	2	3	1½	2	4	190
18	2½	3	2	2½	4	213
20	2½	3½	2	2½	4	237
22	3	4	2½	3	5	260
24	3	4	2½	3	5	285

ESTIMATING DRYWALL QUANTITIES

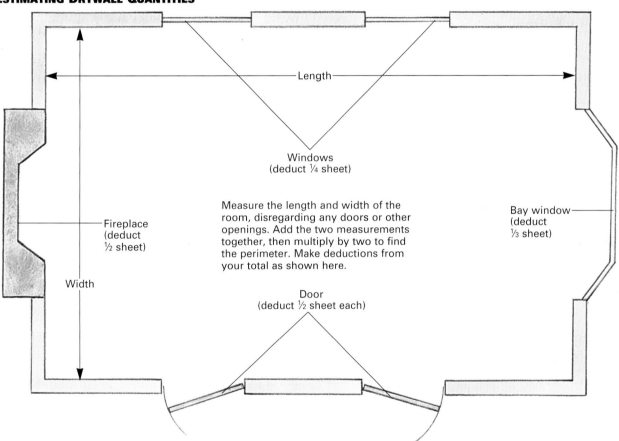

Length

Windows (deduct ¼ sheet)

Measure the length and width of the room, disregarding any doors or other openings. Add the two measurements together, then multiply by two to find the perimeter. Make deductions from your total as shown here.

Bay window (deduct ⅓ sheet)

Fireplace (deduct ½ sheet)

Width

Door (deduct ½ sheet each)

Recenter the block of full tiles, then redraw the edge tiles. Count all the tiles—including the borders—as full tiles. Order the number of boxes that will give you this quantity, plus an extra box to allow for errors. Before you install the tiles on the floor, lay them in a dry run as shown on page 78 so the layout conforms to your drawing.

ESTIMATING DRYWALL

To estimate the number of 4×8 drywall sheets you'll need, find the total length of the room's

perimeter, divide the result by four, and round the answer up to the nearest whole number. Deduct the amounts shown in the illustration at right for doors and windows, and round the result up to the nearest whole sheet.

To estimate the number of sheets for a ceiling, divide the width of the room by 4 and the length by 8. Round both numbers up and multiply them together to get the number of sheets. Order a few extra sheets to allow for damage and cutting errors.

INSTALLING PARQUET OR VINYL TILE

Wood parquet and resilient tile adhere to the floor with mastic, so installation methods are the same. The only differences are the type of mastic needed and the notch size of the trowel. Make sure the floor is properly prepared (see pages 32–35) and follow these steps:

STANDARD LAYOUT

To lay out perpendicular lines, snap lines between the midpoints of facing walls and square them to each other. Dry-lay tile in both directions to center the layout, then snap new chalk lines.

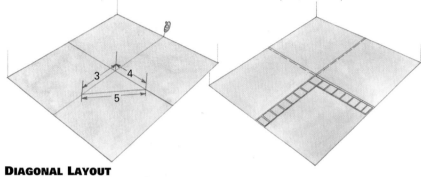

DIAGONAL LAYOUT

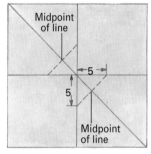
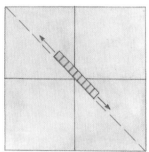

Midpoint of line

5

5

Midpoint of line

Lay out perpendicular lines and snap a diagonal line as shown. Dry-lay tile along a diagonal and shift the tiles to leave even spaces at the corners. Snap a line perpendicular to the diagonal at the center of the tile layout.

TILE LAYOUT

Although you can start your tile layout along any wall that is square to the room, laying out quadrants as shown below will allow you to center the design in the room, leaving even spaces at the walls. For durability and appearance, arrange your layout so that full tiles extend into doorways.

■ Start by snapping chalk lines at the midpoints of opposite walls. If the area is irregular, mark the lines on the largest rectangular portion of the floor.

■ Make sure the intersection of the lines forms a perfect right angle by using the 3-4-5 triangular method: Measure and mark a point 3 feet from the intersection on one axis and 4 feet from the intersection on the other axis. Now measure the distance between the two points. If it's exactly 5 feet, your lines are square. If the intersection is not square, adjust the lines until they meet at 90 degrees.

■ Next, test the layout by dry-laying tiles along the lines in both directions. Start with the line that runs to a doorway and slide the tiles so that you have a full tile at the opening and equal spaces at least

INSTALLING RESILIENT TILE

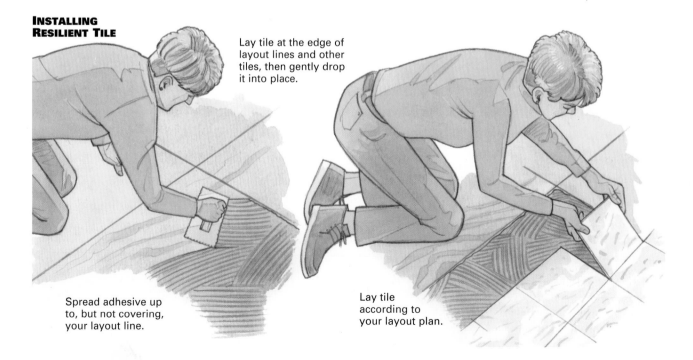

Lay tile at the edge of layout lines and other tiles, then gently drop it into place.

Spread adhesive up to, but not covering, your layout line.

Lay tile according to your layout plan.

half a tile wide on opposite walls. Remark the final layout lines and test them again for square.

SETTING THE FIRST QUADRANT

All adhesives have a specific open time—the length of time from spreading the adhesive until it starts to cure. Tiles won't adhere properly to adhesive after its open time; apply only as much adhesive as you can cover in that time.

■ Starting at the intersection of your layout lines, put a small amount of adhesive on the floor. Then, holding the trowel at a 30- to 45-degree angle, spread the adhesive with the smooth edge of the trowel. Don't cover the layout lines. Strike a balance between spreading it too thick (which will cause it to ooze out between the tiles) and spreading it too thin (which will prevent a good bond). Then comb the adhesive into ridges with the notched side of the trowel.

■ Holding the first tile by the edges, set a corner at the intersection of the layout lines; lower the tile so it's perfectly aligned with the lines. Set the next few tiles along each axis in the same way, tilting the tongue of parquet tiles into the grooves as you set them into the adhesive. Then fill in the area between.

■ Set the tiles in place; sliding them gets mastic on their edges and faces. If you do get mastic on the surface of the tile, wipe it immediately—but gently—with a rag dampened with the solvent specified by the manufacturer. Work carefully to keep each tile squarely aligned with the adjacent one. Minor errors grow as you lay subsequent tiles.

■ Continue laying tiles along each axis and filling in the area between them.

■ When you reach walls or other obstructions, mark and cut the tile (cut parquet with a fine-toothed backsaw and resilient tile with a utility knife), as shown in the illustration below. Resilient tile is brittle when cold; warm the tile with a hair dryer to make cutting easier.

FINISHING THE REMAINING QUADRANTS

When the first quadrant is done, wait until the adhesive cures before laying the other quadrants. Or, you can lay 2×2-foot pieces of plywood on the newly laid tiles so you can walk on them to lay more tile. Start again in the center of the room and use the same methods for the remaining quadrants.

Don't walk directly on the tiles until the adhesive has cured. If you lay parquet, fill the gap at the walls with cork to keep the tiles from shifting.

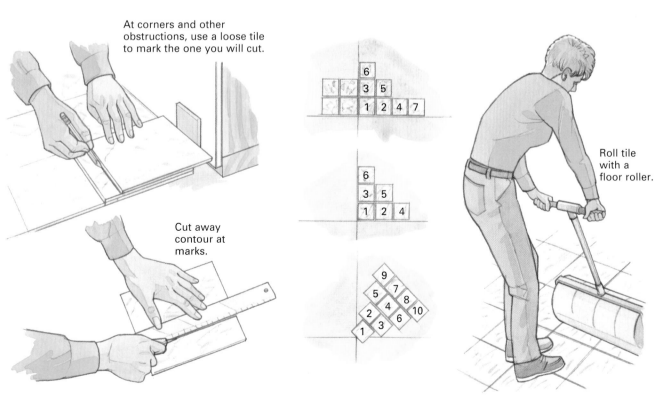

At corners and other obstructions, use a loose tile to mark the one you will cut.

Cut away contour at marks.

Roll tile with a floor roller.

INSTALLING A FLOATING FLOOR

New manufactured or laminate flooring products can be installed without attaching them to the subfloor. Manufactured wood flooring is made with a real wood wear layer on top of a number of plies of hardwood. Some of these products are glued directly to the floor, but others are suitable for floating.

Laminate flooring materials have a tough synthetic wear layer bonded to medium-density fiberboard. Manufactured wood and laminate flooring are held together with glued edges. Prepare the subfloor as specified by the manufacturer, and start laying the flooring by putting down the underlayment.

FOAM UNDERLAYMENT

Start in a corner and butt the end of the underlayment against one wall. Unroll it to the opposite wall and cut the end to fit. Some manufacturers recommend installing a section of flooring after laying the first course of underlayment. If that's what you have, proceed to the next step ("Dry-Laying the Planks") and go on to lay the flooring. Then, alternately lay underlayment and flooring.

Otherwise, continue unrolling the underlayment until you've covered the entire floor surface. Butt the pieces together; don't overlap them. Tape the seams together unless the manufacturer recommends against it. For solid-panel underlayment, follow the manufacturer's instructions. Solid panels usually require a ¼-inch gap for expansion.

TIPS FOR GLUING

Manufactured wood and laminate flooring products vary widely in their gluing requirements. Some manufacturers recommend applying glue to the tongue of the planks. Others specify gluing the groove. Still others specify gluing both the tongue and the groove. Be sure to follow the directions for your flooring and use only the glue recommended by the manufacturer. If you don't follow the procedures specified or you use the wrong kind of glue, you might void the product warranty.

All manufacturers make the same recommendation on how much glue to apply. Properly applied glue will ooze slightly from the joint when pressure is applied with a pull bar or clamp. Too little glue results in a weak bond. Too much will keep the boards from coming together fully. Experiment with scrap pieces before you glue the planks.

INSTALLING A FLOATING FLOOR

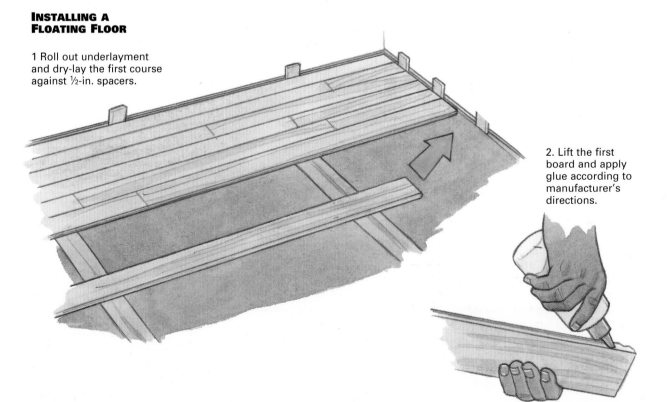

1 Roll out underlayment and dry-lay the first course against ½-in. spacers.

2. Lift the first board and apply glue according to manufacturer's directions.

DRY-LAYING THE PLANKS

Set the first course against ½-inch plywood spacers along the wall. Lay the planks from one sidewall to the other, marking the last plank so you can cut it to fit. Transfer the mark to the back of the plank and cut the plank using a circular saw with a carbide-tipped blade. Turn the plank facedown when cutting. Set this plank in place and pull it snug with a pry bar.

Measure from the opposite wall to both ends of the first course and to the middle. Divide all three measurements by the width of a plank; if you have a remainder of more than 2 inches, dry-lay two more rows, closely following the manufacturer's instructions for staggering the joints.

If the result of the division doesn't leave at least a 2-inch plank on the opposite wall, split the difference and trim the first course narrower so you will have at least 2 inches of material along the starting and ending wall. Then dry-lay two more rows.

GLUING THE EDGES

After dry-laying three courses, it's time to glue. Take up all the planks except the first one, keeping them in order; number them on the back so you can reinstall them in the order they were dry-laid. Apply the glue as recommended by the manufacturer—some products require glue in the tongue, others in the groove, others on both surfaces.

Set the planks back on the underlayment, pushing the tongues into the grooves and immediately wiping up excess glue. Tap the planks together with a piece of flooring scrap and clamp them if required. Continue to dry-lay, glue, and clamp, starting each row with the piece left over from the previous one if it's at least a foot long.

THE LAST COURSE

Set the first plank of the last course along the edge of the wall and mark its width. Transfer the mark to the back of the plank and rip it with a circular saw. Mark and cut each succeeding plank in the same way. Don't cut them all to the same width unless you're sure the wall is square to the floor. Glue the edges of each plank. Set the planks in place, and pull them tight against the rest of the flooring with a pull bar or a pry bar leveraged against the wall with a piece of scrap.

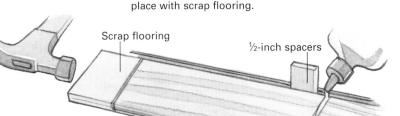

3. Snug each glued board into place with scrap flooring.

Scrap flooring

½-inch spacers

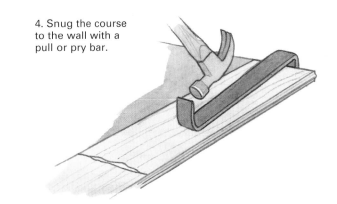

4. Snug the course to the wall with a pull or pry bar.

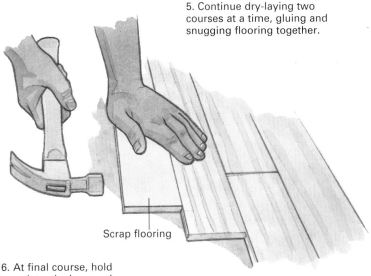

5. Continue dry-laying two courses at a time, gluing and snugging flooring together.

Scrap flooring

6. At final course, hold template plank securely against wall and mark final course for cutting. Cut and install.

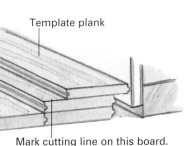

Template plank

Mark cutting line on this board.

INSTALLING SHEET VINYL

MAKING A PAPER TEMPLATE

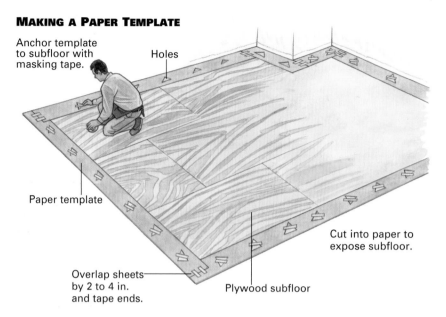

Anchor template to subfloor with masking tape.

Holes

Paper template

Cut into paper to expose subfloor.

Overlap sheets by 2 to 4 in. and tape ends.

Plywood subfloor

S heet vinyl flooring comes in two types: one is installed with adhesive spread on the entire floor, the other with adhesive at the edges only. Both types require proper surface preparation, generally ⁵/₁₆-inch lauan plywood with all gaps and holes filled so the surface is perfectly smooth.

Unroll the sheet in a different room so it relaxes at room temperature for several hours before you cut it. While it's adjusting to the environment of your home, cut a paper template that you will use to cut the flooring.

TRIMMING RESILIENT SHEET FLOORING TO FIT

Cut away on line around perimeter.

Tape seam securely.

Paper template

Chalk line marks seam cut.

Mark perimeter of template on sheet.

Overlap seam edges 3 in.

CUTTING A TEMPLATE

A paper template is a full-sized pattern that you use to cut the sheet flooring to fit the room.
■ Cover the perimeter of the room to within ¼ inch of walls and obstacles with pieces of kraft paper, heavy butcher's paper, or 15-pound felt paper. The heavier the paper, the less it will move around as you work with it. The template doesn't have to fit the room precisely; baseboards and shoe moldings will cover the edges.
■ Overlap the edges of the paper by 2 inches and tape them with heavy tape, such as duct tape. Then cut out small triangles over the surface every 2 feet or so. Put tape over the triangles to hold the template to the subfloor below.
■ With the template taped firmly in place, hold a long straightedge on the edge of the paper and mark its perimeter on the subfloor with a marker. This line will show you where to set the sheet vinyl when you bring it into the room.
■ Roll up the template carefully and bring it into the room where you left the sheet.

TRIMMING THE SHEET

Before laying the template on the vinyl, adjust any pieces that will be seamed so the pattern lines match. Overlap the edges by 3 inches at seams. Tape the edges of the seam together so they won't move. Then lay out the template on the flooring, making sure it lies on the sheet in the way the sheet will be installed in the room.
■ Line up the edges of the template with pattern lines if possible. That way, they won't look awkward in doorways or along prominent walls. Shift the template on the sheet until it's square to the pattern.
■ Tape the template to the sheet vinyl through the triangular holes and mark its edge on the vinyl with a water-soluble marker (use a grease pencil if the surface is glossy).
■ Roll up the template and dispose of it. Then cut the edges of the sheet vinyl with a utility knife, holding a steel straightedge against the material. Roll up the vinyl (don't fold it) with the pattern side in and take it to the room where you will install it.
■ Starting along the wall with the fewest obstacles, unroll the sheet and slide it under door casings. Tug and shift it into place.

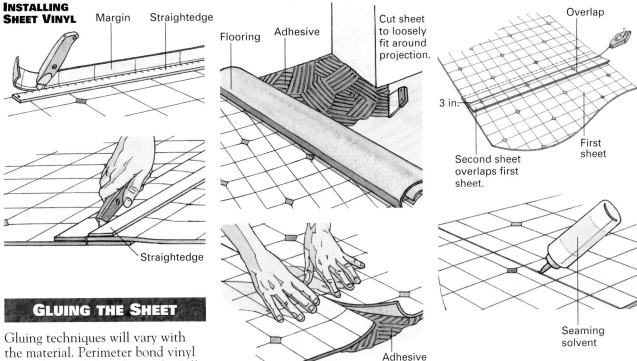

INSTALLING SHEET VINYL — Margin — Straightedge

Straightedge

Flooring — Adhesive — Cut sheet to loosely fit around projection.

Overlap

3 in.

Second sheet overlaps first sheet.

First sheet

Adhesive

Seaming solvent

GLUING THE SHEET

Gluing techniques will vary with the material. Perimeter bond vinyl is glued around the edges only. Full-spread materials are glued to the entire floor surface.

PERIMETER BOND GLUING: Start at a corner. Pull back one edge along a wall, exposing about 8 inches of subfloor, or as much as the manufacturer recommends.
■ Using a ¼-inch notched trowel, spread a band of adhesive on the exposed subfloor. If you will cross a seam location, stop the adhesive about 18 inches from the seam line.
■ Ease the edge of the sheet down on the adhesive and roll it with a floor roller. Then pull back the other edges of the sheet and repeat the procedures along each wall.
■ Seam the sheet, following the procedures shown above right.
■ Staple the edges to the subfloor if required, keeping the staples close to the wall so they will be hidden by the base trim.

FULL-SPREAD VINYL: Carefully lift up half of the sheet and fold it back on the other half without creasing it.
■ Spread adhesive with a ¼-inch notched trowel, working from the corners to the center until you've covered the exposed subfloor. Stop applying adhesive about 18 inches from any seam lines.
■ Fold the sheet back onto the adhesive and roll it from the center to the edges. Then adhere the other half of the floor following the same procedures.

SEAMING SHEET VINYL

Snap a chalk line down the center of the seam overlap.
■ Using a steel straightedge and a sharp utility knife, cut both layers of vinyl along the seam line. Don't cut twice—you'll leave gaps.
■ Pull back both edges and apply adhesive to the floor. Then press both sides of the seam into the adhesive and clean the seam.
■ When the seam has set up, seal it with seaming solvent—it fuses the edges together.

REPAIRING SHEET VINYL

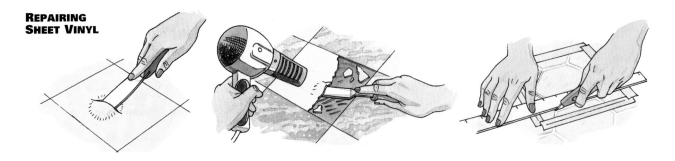

INSTALLING CONVENTIONAL CARPET

Conventional carpet has a fiber backing and requires a pad under it. It is stretched during installation, then held in place by tackless strips nailed along the edge of the floor. Homeowners often hire professional installers to lay carpet, but you can rent the tools and do it yourself.

TACKLESS STRIPS

Tackless strip is thin wood with pointed teeth embedded in it. The teeth point to the wall and hold the carpet in place. Installing it is the first step in laying the carpet.
■ Start in one corner and nail the strip all around the edges of the room, leaving a gap at the wall equal to two-thirds of the carpet thickness. Cut the strips with tin snips and fasten them to the subfloor with at least two nails per section.

PADDING THE FLOOR

Unroll a strip of pad in the room and cut it with a utility knife.
■ On a wood subfloor, staple the pad every 6 to 12 inches. On concrete, tape it with double-faced carpet tape all along its edges.
■ Butt succeeding strips together and tape the joints with duct tape.
■ Trim the pad ¼ inch back from the tackless strip to keep it from riding over the strip when the carpet is stretched.
■ Snap chalk lines on the pad at seams.

CUTTING THE CARPET

For loop pile carpet, use a screwdriver to mark a cutting path and cut from the face side with a utility knife. Cut other carpet from the back.
■ First, measure the piece and mark both edges on the face of the carpet.
■ Roll the carpet back; snap a chalk line on the back side between your marks.
■ Using a long straightedge, cut the back of the carpet with a utility knife, just deep enough to sever the backing. Pull the pieces apart carefully, snipping unseparated threads.

THE ROUGH FIT

Measure and cut carpet sections, leaving a 4- to 6-inch surplus along each wall and a 3-inch overlap at seams. Square the sections to the room and slit the corners so they will lie flat. Now you're ready to seam the carpet and stretch it.

SEAMING THE CARPET

For loop pile carpet, first align the seam edges parallel to each other. Place a straightedge on the edge of the top section and cut the bottom piece with a row cutter. At the wall, cut the surplus with a utility knife.

For other carpet styles, fold back the overlap and snap a chalk line on the back at the seam edges. Cut the line with a utility knife and straightedge.

INSTALLING TACKLESS STRIP AND PAD

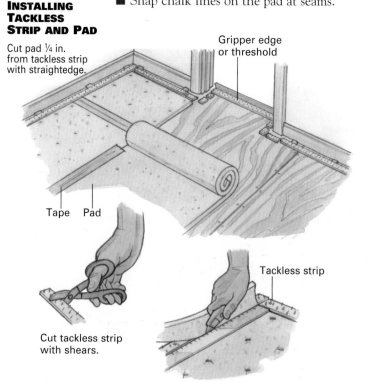

Cut pad ¼ in. from tackless strip with straightedge.

Gripper edge or threshold

Tape   Pad

Tackless strip

Cut tackless strip with shears.

COMPARISON OF CARPET MATERIALS		
Material	**Resilience**	**Wear resistance**
Wool	Excellent; feels springy underfoot.	Very good
Nylon	Very good; resists crushing.	Very good
Polyester	Fair; susceptible to crushing.	Excellent
Acrylic	Good; almost as springy as wool.	Poor
Polypropylene olefin	Varies with construction and type of pile.	Very good

Cut hot-melt seaming tape to the exact length of the seam and center the tape under the seam, adhesive side up. Slip the seaming iron onto the tape at one end of the carpet and let both sides flop onto the iron. Glide the iron slowly along the tape, pressing the seam edges together behind it as you go.

At the wall, stop and let everything cool for 10 minutes. Then roll the surplus carpet back to expose the unheated tape. Heat it and finish the seam by cutting off stray backing or loose pile ends with small scissors.

STRETCHING CARPET

Carpet stretchers need adjustment before you use them. Adjust the bite of both the knee kicker and power stretcher until the teeth just grab the backing without poking through it.

To use the knee kicker, bite the head into the carpet about 1 inch from the wall. Push down on the handle and give the cushion a swift kick with your knee. Push down the surplus carpet at the wall with a stair tool.

To use the power stretcher, set the head about 6 inches away from the wall and adjust the extension tubes so the foot pushes against a piece of 2×4 (make it long enough to span three studs) at the other wall. Press the lever until it locks.

Stretching normally begins in a corner by an entrance and proceeds along both sides of the opening for about 3 feet. Then power stretch one corner at a time, knee kicking along each length in turn. Follow the directions for the style you have purchased.

TRIMMING

Always trim the carpet edges with a wall trimmer, not a utility knife. Adjust the trimmer for the thickness of the carpet. Start at the lapped end of the material and slice downward at an angle until the trimmer is flat against the floor. Then hold the trimmer against both the wall and the floor and plow along the edge of the wall.

When you're stopped by the wall, trim the last few inches with a utility knife and tuck the trimmed edge into the gap with a stair tool.

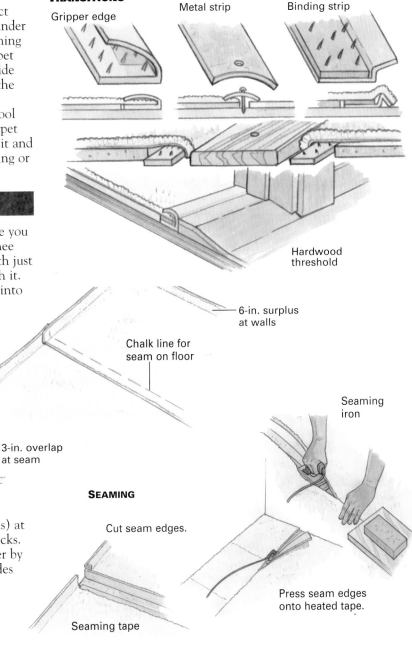

TRANSITIONS

Gripper edge

Metal strip

Binding strip

Hardwood threshold

6-in. surplus at walls

Chalk line for seam on floor

LAYOUT

3-in. overlap at seam

SEAMING

Cut seam edges.

Seaming tape

Seaming iron

Press seam edges onto heated tape.

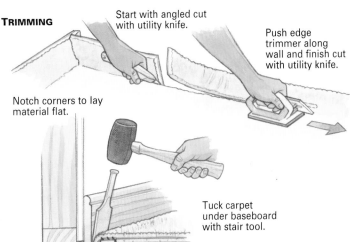

TRIMMING

Start with angled cut with utility knife.

Push edge trimmer along wall and finish cut with utility knife.

Notch corners to lay material flat.

Tuck carpet under baseboard with stair tool.

INSTALLING DRYWALL

DRYWALL INSTALLATION

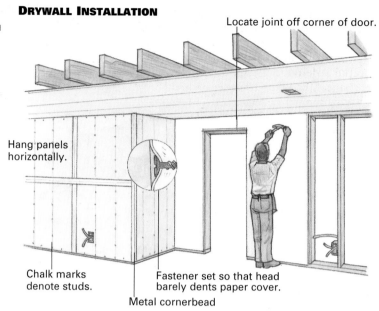

Locate joint off corner of door.

Hang panels horizontally.

Chalk marks denote studs.

Fastener set so that head barely dents paper cover.

Metal cornerbead

Hanging drywall requires more strength than skill, but if you haven't done it before, taping and finishing the joints may be challenging. Practice on scrap before starting the walls.

PREPARATION

You'll save a lot of time hanging the drywall if you plan your layout in advance. Sketch the room and mark in the position of the panels. You can hang them horizontally or vertically, but taping will be easier if you hang them horizontally—you'll have one long waist-high joint to tape instead of several vertical ones.

Use full sheets when possible, and position joints at doorways on a central stud so they don't coincide with the framing corners. Panels are usually 4×8 feet, but larger sizes (4×10, 12, and 14 feet) are available. If the longer lengths fit the dimensions of your walls better (and you can handle the larger sheets), you'll have fewer seams.

If you have framed the room with kiln-dried lumber, you shouldn't have problems from nails popping out as the framing dries. Green lumber shrinks as it dries, but you can

DRYWALL FASTENERS

The drywall screw (type W screw) has proven so technically superior in nearly every carpentry situation that we often ignore other wallboard fasteners.

Fasteners	Application
Ringshank nail	Single layer of wallboard to wood framing.
Cup-head nail	Single layer of wallboard to wood framing.
Type S screw	Wallboard to sheet-metal studs or furring.
Type G screw	Wallboard to wallboard or wood framing.

CUTTING DRYWALL

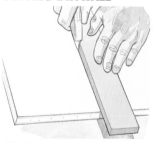

Mark a straight cut and cut through the good side with a utility knife and a straightedge.

Turn the board over, lift the smaller segment up, and cut through the crease with the knife.

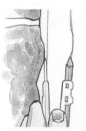

To mark an irregular cut, set a drawing compass to about 1 inch and trace the shape while holding the compass legs horizontal.

To make holes, cut through the paper on all four sides and diagonally.

Strike the center of the X with a hammer; the drywall will break into four triangular tabs.

Turn the board over, raise the tabs, and cut along the creases to remove the tabs.

minimize nail popping by closing up the room for about a week before hanging the drywall and by keeping the temperature at 72 degrees.

If you will start the job soon after the material is delivered, stack the panels against the last wall you plan to cover so you'll have plenty of floor space to maneuver the panels and cut them. If you have to wait to hang the panels, stack them on the floor to keep them from developing sags.

You'll save time and avoid much of the dust that accompanies dry sanding if you use joint compound that can be sanded wet.

PUTTING UP THE CEILING

Install the ceiling first, marking the joist centers on the wall so you can tell where the fasteners go.
■ Start on one wall and lift the panel into place, holding the opposite end with a T brace. Make sure to position the panel so its outside edge is centered on a joist.
■ Start fastening in the center of the panel, spacing nails at 8 inches, screws at 12 inches. Drive them just until they dimple—not punch through—the paper cover. When you reach an end, keep the fastener at least ⅜ inch from it.
■ Measure, cut, and fasten the remaining panels, keeping cut ends against the wall and leaving a small gap.

HANGING WALL PANELS

Mark the centers of studs on the ceiling so you can tell where to drive the fasteners.
■ If you're hanging panels horizontally, the top one goes first—snug against the ceiling. Brace it in place until it's fastened, and drive fasteners as described for ceiling panels.
■ Snug the lower panel against the upper one, supporting it with a piece of scrap plywood pivoted on a dowel or 1× scrap. Fill in any gaps at the bottom with drywall strips—they will be covered by the baseboard.
■ When you have to cut a piece to fit, cut it slightly smaller than the opening so you'll have enough clearance. Jamming drywall pieces together will break the edges and make it difficult to tape a finished-looking joint.
■ Avoid using construction cement without fasteners. The cement adheres only to the paper backing and the backing will pull away from the drywall if moisture or temperature causes any expansion or contraction.

FINISHING

Follow the finishing steps shown at right, making sure each coat of compound is thoroughly dry before applying the next one.

INSTALLING CEILING PANELS

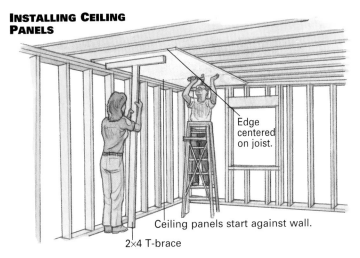

Edge centered on joist.

Ceiling panels start against wall.

2×4 T-brace

TAPING AND FINISHING SEAMS

1. Spread a layer of compound along the entire length of a joint.

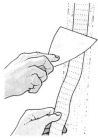

2. Lay tape in wet compound and smooth with a 3- or 4-in. knife.

3. With a 4-in. knife, apply a thin layer of compound. Feather the edges carefully.

4. Fill and smooth all dimples with a layer of compound.

5. Let compound dry, then sand. Or, moisten it with a wet sponge and smooth it with a 4-in. knife.

6. Apply a second coat. Smooth and feather joint with a 6-in. knife. Sand when dry. Repeat with a third coat.

OUTSIDE CORNERS

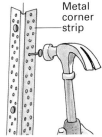

Metal corner strip

1. Nail metal corner strip to fit smoothly and tightly.

2. Apply compound with a putty knife or a corner trowel.

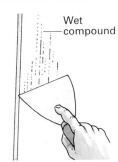

Wet compound

3. Finish in the same way as for a taped joint.

PANELING OPTIONS

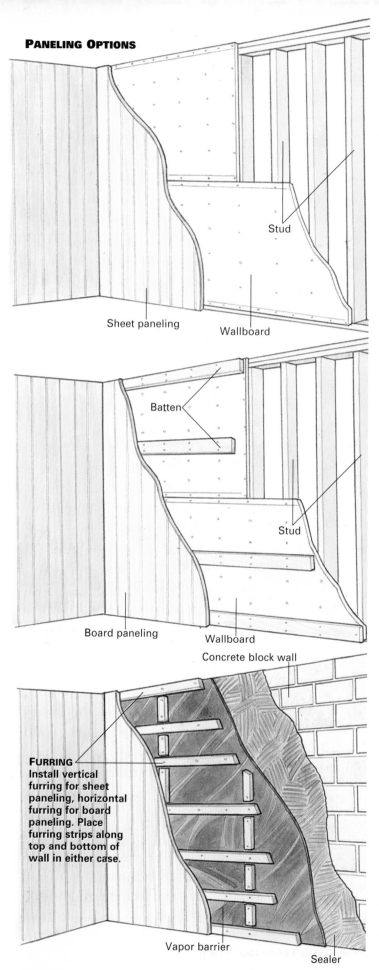

Sheet paneling

Stud

Wallboard

Batten

Stud

Board paneling

Wallboard

Concrete block wall

FURRING
Install vertical
furring for sheet
paneling, horizontal
furring for board
paneling. Place
furring strips along
top and bottom of
wall in either case.

Vapor barrier

Sealer

INSTALLING WOOD PANELING

W ood paneling offers more design choices than many other wall finishings. Tongue-and-groove material is available in pine, redwood, cedar, oak, and mahogany; some styles come in planks with vertical grooves that give it the look of several narrower strips. Still others come prefinished.

Sheet paneling is made in two types: plywood with a wood-veneer face and hardboard covered with printed paper or vinyl.

PREPARING FOR SHEET PANELS

Sheet panels go up quickly with proper preparation. Start by checking the wall for level. First, check the wall with a 4-foot level. If all areas are within ¼ inch of the same flat plane, you can proceed. If the wall is not level, nail 1×2s every 24 inches at points where the panels will join.

Over exposed studs, hang ½-inch drywall to provide a solid surface behind the thin paneling. Most codes require fire-resistant drywall behind paneling.

If you're working on a concrete block wall, seal it with concrete sealer, cover it with 6-mil polyethylene sheets, and fur it out with 1×3 furring strips (see illustration at left), shimming them to keep the surface level.

Adding furring strips to an existing wall may extend the wall beyond the trim, but you can even things up with jamb extensions. Remove the trim carefully and rip pieces of 1× or 2× stock to match the new wall thickness. Nail them to the door or window jambs and replace the trim when the paneling is installed.

INSTALLING SHEET PANELING

Bring the panels inside several days before hanging. Store them flat on the floor and let them become acclimated to your home.

Install the first panel in an unobstructed corner, plumbing it with a 4-foot level and centering it on a stud or furring strip. Fasten the panel every 8 inches with nails that will penetrate the studs or furring strips by at least ¾ inch. If you're using panel adhesive, run a bead on every nailing surface. Following the manufacturer's instructions, hang the panel, nailing it at the top and bottom.

When you meet an obstruction or a corner of the room that is not plumb, butt the panel against the obstruction, plumb with a panel already in place. Use a compass or scribing tool to mark the outline of the obstruction; plan the width of the cut so the edge of the panel will butt up against the adjacent panel.

When cutting paneling, use a fine-toothed blade (12 teeth to the inch for a handsaw, a plywood blade for a power saw) to avoid tearing up the edges. Cut paneling faceup with a handsaw or a table saw, facedown with a radial arm or circular saw. Don't use a saber saw when cutting panels.

INSTALLING TONGUE-AND-GROOVE PANELING

Tongue-and-groove paneling is usually installed over horizontal battens.

If you're working on a finished wall, nail 1×3 battens at the top and bottom of the wall and at 32 and 64 inches from the floor. Pry off the trim and cut and fasten jamb extenders to the door and window frames.

If you're hanging the paneling on an exposed stud wall, snap chalk lines across the studs at these measurements. With a circular saw set to $1\frac{1}{2}$ inches and a chisel, form recesses in the studs for 1×3 battens. Nail the battens with 8d nails, flush with the surface of the studs. Then mark the location of the battens on adjacent walls and cover them with $\frac{1}{2}$-inch drywall.

Bring the boards into the room and lay them out for three days to a week so they become acclimated to your home.

Hang the first board plumb, scribing it if necessary. Facenail it to the battens with the tongue out and blindnail the tongue at a 45-degree angle. Fit the groove of the next board into the tongue and tap it snug with

TYPES OF PANELING

Type	Thickness	Cost	Description
Hardboard	$\frac{1}{8}$ and $\frac{1}{4}$ in.	Low	Compressed and glued fibers, with a paper or plastic facing which is often printed to simulate real wood; fairly water-resistant; easy to install.
Plywood	$\frac{1}{8}$, $\frac{5}{32}$, and $\frac{3}{16}$ in.	Medium	Three wood plies; face veneer high quality soft- or hardwood; grooved to resemble boards; water-resistant; easy to install.
Boards	$\frac{3}{8}$ and $\frac{3}{4}$ in.	High	Solid wood; edges may be plain, shiplapped, or tongue-and-groove; installation requires more time; extremely durable.

a piece of panel scrap. Then blindnail the tongue. At every third board, check your alignment for plumb. Continue nailing panels and checking for plumb until you reach the opposite wall.

You may have to cut the final board to fit. Measure from the wall to the inside of the tongue of the next-to-last board. Measure in several places and mark the longest measurement at the tongue side of the top of the last board. Now hold the last board to the wall, keeping it plumb, and set your compass to the distance between the mark and the wall. Scribe along the entire length of the board, then cut along that line. Test-fit the board and cut the rear edge of the groove if necessary so it will fall in place. Facenail the last board to the battens.

SCRIBING PANELING

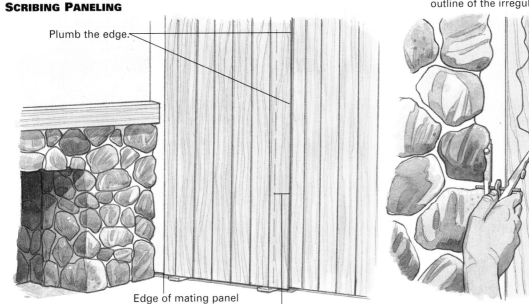

Plumb the edge.

Hold the compass level as you trace the outline of the irregular wall onto paneling.

Edge of mating panel

Open the compass to this distance (amount of overlap) for scribing.

FINISHING THE CEILING

INSTALLING CEILING TILE

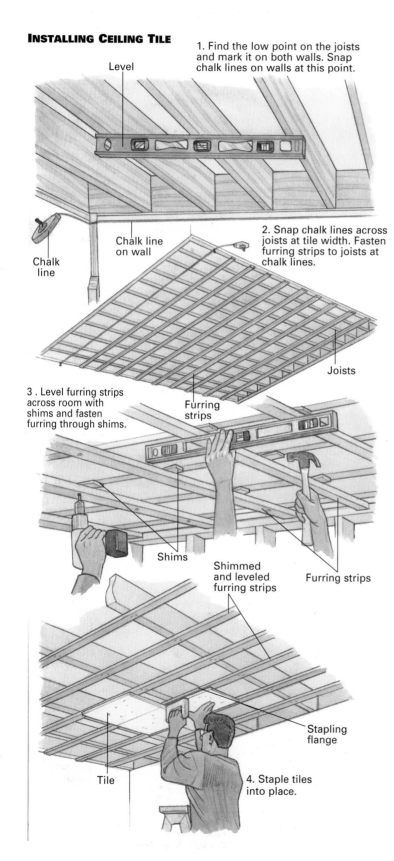

1. Find the low point on the joists and mark it on both walls. Snap chalk lines on walls at this point.

Level

Chalk line on wall

Chalk line

2. Snap chalk lines across joists at tile width. Fasten furring strips to joists at chalk lines.

Joists

3. Level furring strips across room with shims and fasten furring through shims.

Furring strips

Shims

Shimmed and leveled furring strips

Furring strips

Stapling flange

Tile

4. Staple tiles into place.

Before installing a tiled or suspended ceiling, install wiring and boxes for any ceiling fixtures. Recessed fixtures ordinarily require 8 inches of clearance. Flush-mounted fixtures should match the style of the surrounding materials.

TILING A CEILING

Although there are many styles and sizes of ceiling tile, most are made of either organic fibers or mineral fibers. Organic tiles are normally ½-inch thick. Mineral-fiber tiles are fireproof and are usually ¾-inch thick. Both come in 12- or 24-inch squares.

The size you use will partly depend on the size of the room. Large tiles go up faster because each tile covers more area, but large tiles may overwhelm a small space. If you're in doubt, get a couple of samples of each size and try them on the ceiling before making your purchase.

If you're tiling an existing finished ceiling, check it with a long straightedge to see how flat it is. You can adhere tile to a finished ceiling with construction or tiling adhesive, but the surface must be smooth and absolutely flat. Most ceilings aren't, so you'll need to level the surface with 1×3s, shimming them to provide a flat surface.

■ Snap chalk lines at the midpoints of opposing walls. Measure from the midpoint along both axes and adjust the lines until you have evenly cut tiles along all the walls.

■ Center your first furring strip on your final line and space the remaining strips at the width of the tiles.

■ Starting in the center, staple (with two staples on each edge) or glue the tiles into place. Install the four center tiles and work outward in all directions.

■ When you reach the walls, use a utility knife to cut each end tile separately so it fits any unevenness in the wall.

If you're tiling over exposed joists, use the same procedures above to locate and fasten furring strips to the joists. Then proceed in the same manner to nail or glue the tiles to the furring strips.

SUSPENDING A CEILING

Suspended ceilings offer several advantages. They hide cracks or other imperfections in an existing finished ceiling, they conceal ductwork and wiring in a basement, and they cover sagging or uneven joists. The support members (both exposed and hidden) and the acoustic tile inserts come in a variety of colors and textures to match almost any decorating scheme. Before you start, insulate cold water pipes to prevent drips from condensation.

■ Suspending a ceiling begins with marking chalk lines on the walls at the height of the finished surface—at least 7½ feet above the finished floor. Measure this distance and use a water level to mark the walls. Then snap chalk lines between the marks.

■ Nail the edge support strip along the lines. Snip it if it buckles from unevenness in the wall, and nail it on both sides of the cut.

■ Mark the edge support at the dimensions of the tile inserts—usually 2×2 or 2×4—and run a level string from one wall to the other at the bottom of the edge support.

■ At each mark, measure the length for the main supports (they will probably be different lengths at different locations) and cut them with snips. As you cut the main supports, make sure the slots for the cross members line up with the dimensions of your inserts.

■ Working with a helper, suspend the main runners from screw eyes and wires (or whatever hardware is supplied with the materials) looped through holes in the runner flange. Tighten the wire so the runner is level with the string along its entire length.

■ Now install the cross runners and measure the diagonals of each section to make sure they are square. If any section is out of square, snip off a section of the cross runner and bring it into alignment.

■ Tilt the tile inserts into the opening of the grid, set one edge on a runner, and let the insert fall into place. Push the runner snug against the tile.

BOXING OBSTRUCTIONS

When suspending a ceiling in a basement, you may find that windows don't fit well with your evenly spaced layout. You can readjust the position of the entire grid, but that'll probably cause an inequity somewhere else in the room.

If you have this problem, install the entire grid as described above, then build a box from aluminum fascia, bending square corners by snipping the flange. Set the box in the grid and fasten it to the support member with pop rivets. Fasten a piece of edge support to the joist above the window and to the box on the opposite side. Tilt cut panels into place.

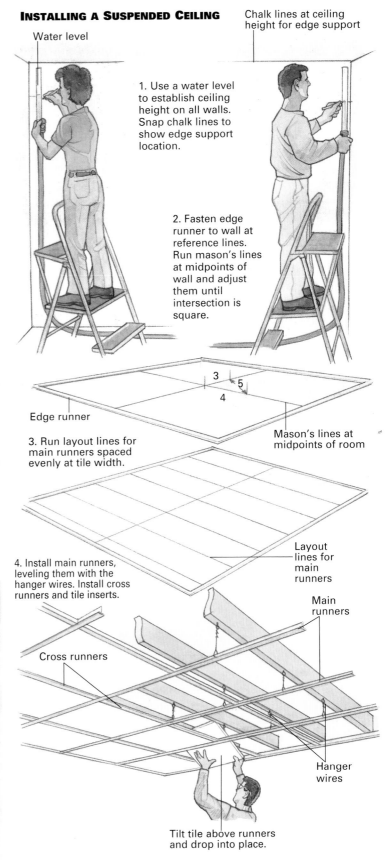

INSTALLING A SUSPENDED CEILING

Water level

Chalk lines at ceiling height for edge support

1. Use a water level to establish ceiling height on all walls. Snap chalk lines to show edge support location.

2. Fasten edge runner to wall at reference lines. Run mason's lines at midpoints of wall and adjust them until intersection is square.

Edge runner

3 5 4

Mason's lines at midpoints of room

3. Run layout lines for main runners spaced evenly at tile width.

Layout lines for main runners

Main runners

4. Install main runners, leveling them with the hanger wires. Install cross runners and tile inserts.

Cross runners

Hanger wires

Tilt tile above runners and drop into place.

CLOSETS, CABINETS, AND SHELVING

Closet and storage space may have been one of your highest remodeling priorities, but they are among the last tasks to be completed in any project.

Closet framing should be completed along with any other new framing, but it can be done in a finished room also. Cabinets and shelving also go up after you've hung the drywall. All three will be fastened to the wall studs, so in a finished room, you'll start by locating the studs and joists and marking them on the walls and ceilings. Draw vertical plumb lines in the center of the studs for cabinet installation—everything will have to fit exactly.

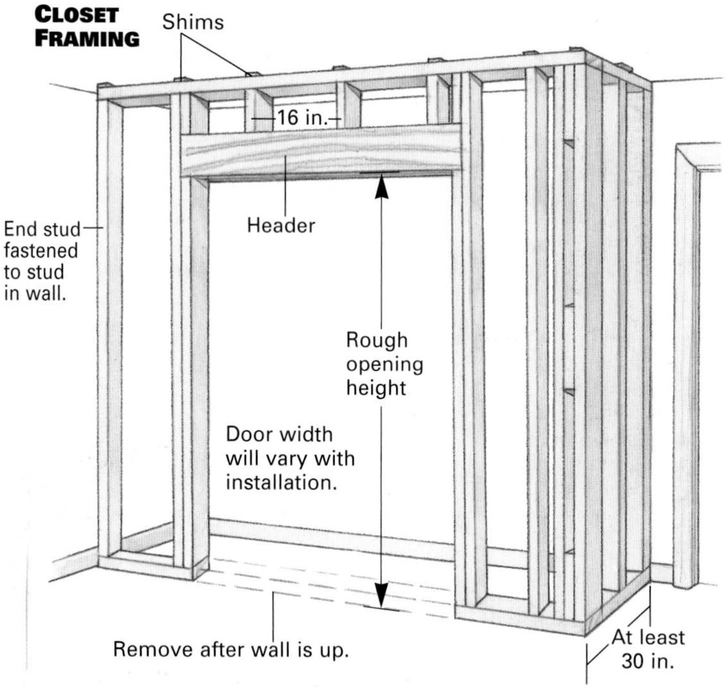

BUILDING A CLOSET

Use these basic dimensions when you plan your closet: For a bedroom closet, allow 4 linear feet of hanging space and 8 square feet of storage for each person. Closet depth should be 24 inches for hangers and shelving at least a foot deep (20 inches is better). The illustration at left shows typical closet framing, but yours can be smaller or larger as your needs dictate.

Using the techniques described on pages 38–39, frame the walls in place, or preassemble them and raise them when they're built. Remember to cut studs ¼ inch shorter than the full wall height if preassembling—that allows enough room to clear the ceiling. Double the corner studs and build the doorway header as you go, but don't cut the bottom plate at the doorway until all the walls are fastened together. Shim the top plate to the ceiling or the joists and nail through the shims. Then finish the framing with drywall or wood paneling.

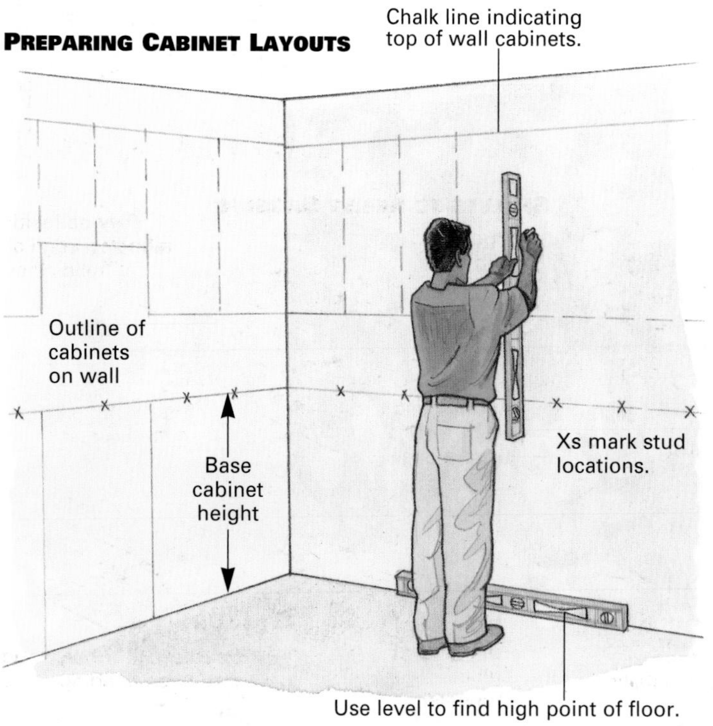

PREPARING FOR CABINETRY

There are lots of decisions to make before installing cabinets. Most of them involve style and layout, and when you've made those decisions, the installation for most styles is basically the same.

The floor in your room may not be perfectly flat; check it along the wall with a level. If you find a high spot, transfer the point to the wall. Mark a heavy horizontal line on the wall 34½ inches up from the high spot. Then mark another line at 36 inches. These lines represents the top of your base cabinets and the top of your countertop. Measure and mark similar lines for the tops of your wall cabinets, normally at 84 inches above the high point of the floor.

Wall cabinets are installed first, except when the countertop backsplash goes up to the wall cabinets or when there is a full-length wall cabinet in the middle of the run. Measure the distance from the edge location to the studs and mark the interior of the cabinets so you'll know where the fasteners go. Predrill and countersink fastener holes along these lines.

CLOSET FRAMING

Shims

16 in.

Header

End stud fastened to stud in wall.

Rough opening height

Door width will vary with installation.

Remove after wall is up.

At least 30 in.

PREPARING CABINET LAYOUTS

Chalk line indicating top of wall cabinets.

Outline of cabinets on wall

Base cabinet height

Xs mark stud locations.

Use level to find high point of floor.

INSTALLING WALL CABINETS

Hanging wall units is a two-person job, so get someone to help. Starting with a corner cabinet, lift the unit into place, support it with a brace, and attach it to the studs with 3-inch drywall screws—but tighten only one of the top screws. Correct any unevenness in the wall with shims at the screws.

Prepare remaining units in the same way, predrilling the sides of the stiles. Then lift each to place and clamp the stiles together so the joint is tight and flush. Fasten the stiles together with 1½-inch drywall screws. At the end of the run, add a filler piece between the last cabinet and the wall if necessary.

INSTALLING BASE CABINETS

Set the base unit into place and shim its bottom edge until the unit is even with the line you marked. Then fasten the unit to the studs with 3-inch drywall screws through predrilled rails. Set the second unit into place, shim it, and clamp and fasten the stiles the same way as for the wall units. Complete the run and fasten the base doors and cabinet top according to the manufacturer's instructions.

SHELVING

Whether you're installing shelves in an open or framed bookcase or hanging them as built-in units, you have a number of choices on how to support them. If you want fixed-

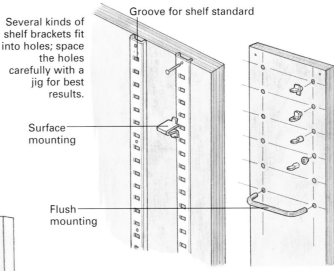

INSTALLING WALL CABINETS

Stiles screwed together

Corner unit

Measure for last cabinet and filler.

C-clamp

T-brace

height, permanent shelving, you can cut dadoes in the sides and back of the unit. For movable shelves, install surface- or flush-mounted brackets, rear-mounted standards, or drill evenly spaced holes for removable clips or dowels. If you drill support holes, mark their locations carefully and drill them with a drill press.

MOUNTING SHELF STANDARDS

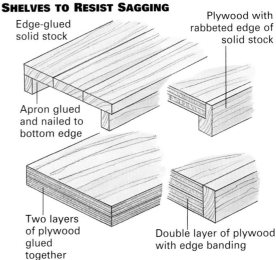

Groove for shelf standard

Several kinds of shelf brackets fit into holes; space the holes carefully with a jig for best results.

Surface mounting

Flush mounting

SHELVES TO RESIST SAGGING

Edge-glued solid stock

Plywood with rabbeted edge of solid stock

Apron glued and nailed to bottom edge

Two layers of plywood glued together

Double layer of plywood with edge banding

INSTALLING BASE CABINETS

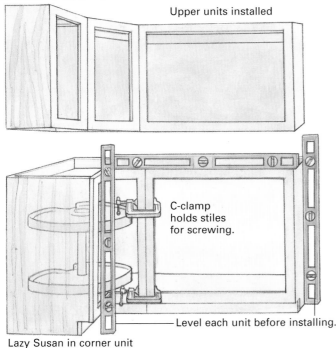

Upper units installed

C-clamp holds stiles for screwing.

Level each unit before installing.

Lazy Susan in corner unit

TRIM WORK

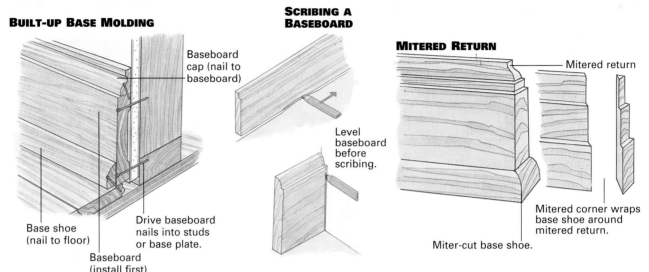

BUILT-UP BASE MOLDING

Baseboard cap (nail to baseboard)

Base shoe (nail to floor)

Drive baseboard nails into studs or base plate.

Baseboard (install first)

SCRIBING A BASEBOARD

Level baseboard before scribing.

MITERED RETURN

Mitered return

Mitered corner wraps base shoe around mitered return.

Miter-cut base shoe.

Trimming your finished room involves installing baseboards and window and door trim. You may have additional trim work in the form of crown molding, chair rails, picture rails, and corner guards, but the techniques for these embellishments are similar. Leave any needed trim work for last. Paint the walls first—or wallpaper them—and save some time by prepainting or finishing the moldings before you attach them.

BASEBOARDS

Baseboards come as one-, two-, or three-piece units with the additional pieces made from standard molding. It's best to have the floor covering in place before attaching the baseboards, but if you don't, allow for its thickness when nailing the baseboard trim. Shoe molding goes on after the finished floor. Make miter cuts at outside corners and use butt joints at inside corners for square-edged stock, coped joints for moldings.

MITERING DOOR AND WINDOW TRIM

Mitered corners add style to trim work and give it a professionally finished look. Start by squaring off one piece of the casing, then hold it against the frame ¼ inch back from the frame edge—an amount called the *reveal*. Mark the point at which the top reveal intersects the casing. From this point, miter the casing at 45 degrees and nail it to the jamb. Cut one end of the head casing at 45 degrees and mark the intersection of the reveal on the other side. Tack the head casing to the frame. Square off the casing on the other side and hold it in place, marking the top and bottom of the head casing miter. Scribe between the marks and cut along the line. Then, nail the casing into place.

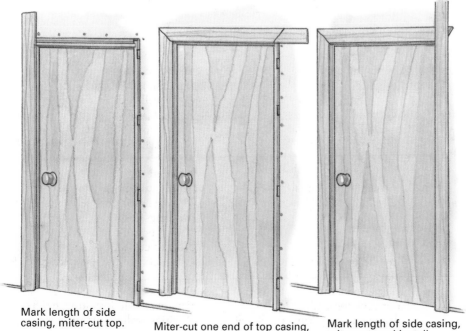

Mark length of side casing, miter-cut top.

Miter-cut one end of top casing, tack in place, mark length, and miter-cut other end.

Mark length of side casing, miter-cut, and install.

INDEX

A–B

Asbestos, danger of, 31
Attics, 50–63
  ceilings, 16, 53
  doors, 60, 61
  dormers, 16, 54–57
  insulating, 21, 63
  joists, 32, 33, 52–53
  leaks, looking for, 23
  running circuit to, 47
  skylights, 4, 10, 22, 62
  stairs, 51
  vents, 21, 63
  walls, building, 58–59
  walls, openings in, 60–61
  windows, 4, 22, 60–61
Basements, 64–75
  doors and doorways, 18, 72, 73, 74
  drains, 21, 68
  enlarging, with new room, 17
  floor preparation, 68–69
  headroom, increasing, 16–17
  insulating, 21
  joists, 32, 33
  moisture in, 23, 65
  stairs, 66–67
  walls, breaching, 72, 73
  walls, building, 70–71
  walls, sealing, 65
  windows, 5, 22, 72, 73, 75
  window wells, 22, 23, 72–73, 74–75
Bathrooms, 11, 68
  fixture rough-in dimensions, 27
Bearing vs. nonbearing walls, 36–37, 70–71
Bedrooms, 4, 8–9
  joist spans for, 32
Bids, obtaining, 29
Block walls
  breaching, 72, 73
  building, 39
Boxed-in ceiling obstructions, 35, 91
Boxes, electrical, 46–47
Budget for remodeling project, 25
Building codes. See Codes, building

C

Cabinets, 92–93
Cable, running, 46, 47
Carpet, 12, 69, 84–85
Casings, door and window, 13, 94
Cathedral ceilings, attic, 53
Ceilings
  attic, 16, 53
  cracks, avoiding, 50
  drywall, installing, 87
  height, 7
  obstructions, boxing in, 35, 91
  suspended, 90–91
  tiles, installing, 90

Cement, hydraulic, use of, 65
Clearances, minimum, 7
  for bathroom fixtures, 11
Closets, 92
Codes, building, 5
  for apartments, 8
  for cable, 47
  for habitable rooms, 7
  for plumbing, 49
  for receptacles, 47
  for stairs, 18, 44, 67
  for wall framing, 37
  for windows, 22, 42
Concrete block walls. See Block walls
Concrete slab floors, 34–35
  preparing, 68–69
Condensation in basement, 23
Contractors, use of, 28–29
Cost of project, 25
  reducing, 26, 28

D

Design decisions, making, 13
Design ideas, 6–11
Design professionals, use of, 26
Dimensioned drawing, 26
Do-it-yourself jobs, 28
Doors and doorways
  attic, 60, 61
  basement, 18, 72, 73, 74
  pocket doors, installing, 41
  prehung doors, installing, 40–41
  rough openings, 38, 40, 61
  trim, 13, 94
Dormers, 16
  gable, 56–57
  shed, 54–55
Drainage systems, 23, 72–73
Drains, 21
  branch line, basement, 68
Drain-waste-vent (DWV) lines, 15, 49
Drywall
  estimating, 77
  installing, 86–87
  removing, 36
  supplies, 77, 86

E–F

Electrical systems, 15, 20, 46–47
Enlargement of space, 16–17
Estimates
  of costs, preparing for, 27
  of finishing materials, 76–77
Excavation around basements, 22, 72–73, 74–75
Fasteners, 30, 31
  drywall, 77, 86
  powder-actuated nailer for, 71
Fiberglass, working with, 63
Flashing, window, 43, 61
Floor coverings, 12, 76–85
  basement, preparing for, 68–69
  carpet, 12, 69, 84–85

  estimating quantities of, 76, 77
  floating floor, 80–81
  sheet vinyl, 82–83
  tile, 12, 77, 78–79
Floor plans, 26–27
Floors, 14, 32–35
  attic, 52–53, 63
  concrete slab, 34–35, 68–69
  joists, 14, 32–33, 52–53
  subfloors, installing, 34, 53, 69
Framing, 14
  attics, 50–62
  closets, 92
  dormers, 54–57
  floors, 32–33, 52–53
  metal, 70
  openings, door and window, 40, 61, 73, 75
  skylights, 62
  stairs, 51, 66, 67
  walls, 37, 38, 39, 46, 58–59, 70–71
Furring strips, use of, 71, 88, 90

G–K

Gable-end walls, openings in, 60–61
Headroom
  basement, increasing, 16–17
  minimum requirements, 7
  stairs, 18, 44
Heat, windows and, 22, 42
Heating and cooling, 20, 21
Hydraulic cement, use of, 65
Inspections, calendar of, 29
Insulation, 21, 63
Joists, 14, 32–33
  attic, 32, 33, 52–53
  and plumbing, 21, 48
  stair opening cut in, 51
Knee walls
  building, 58–59

L–O

Laminate flooring materials, 12, 80
Lead, danger of, 31
Leaks, finding, 23
Lighting plan, 12, 13
Light wells, 22, 73, 74–75
Load-bearing vs. nonbearing walls, 36–37, 70–71
Manufactured wood flooring, 12, 80
Metal frame windows, removing, 42
Metal framing, 70
Miters, cutting, 57, 94
Moisture problems, solving, 23, 65
Moldings, 13, 94
Nailer, powder-actuated, 71
No-hub connectors, 48, 49
Obstructions, ceiling, boxing, 35, 91

P–R

Paneling, wall, installing, 88–89
Partition walls, building, 17

attic, 58, 59, 60
basement, 70–71
Pitch (slope) of roof, 54, 56
Plans, making, 24–29
order of work, 25, 50
Plastic pipe, joining, 48, 49
Platform stairs, building, 66, 67
Plumbing systems, 15, 20–21, 48–49
basement branch drains, 68
fixture rough-in dimensions, 27
Pocket doors, installing, 41
Prehung doors, installing, 40–41
Rafters, 14
and attic ceilings, 53
and dormers, 54, 55, 56, 57
Rafter ties, 14
altering, to raise ceiling, 16
Receptacles, codes for, 47
Resilient flooring, 12, 78–79, 82–83
Ridge beams, 60
Roofs
dormers built in, 54–57
insulating, 63
skylight installation in, 62
trusses, 15
Rooms
habitable, codes for, 7
sizes, recommended, 6

S
Safety, 31
fiberglass, 63
stair angle, 45
Sheet vinyl flooring, 82–83
Shelving, 93

Skylights, 4, 10, 22, 62
codes for, 42
Slab floors, concrete, 34–35
preparing, 68–69
Sleepers, installing, in basement, 69
Slope of roof, 54, 56
Soldering of copper pipe, 49
Spiral and winder stairs, 19, 44
Stairways, 12, 18–19, 44–45
attic, 51
basement, 66–67
codes for, 18, 44, 67
measurements, 18, 44, 45, 66
rebuilding or relocating, 18
Storage, 19, 92–93
Stringers, stair, laying out, 44, 45
Subfloors, installing, 34
attic, 53
basement, 69
Sump pump, installing, 65

T–V
Template, making, for sheet vinyl, 82
Terraced light well, making, 74–75
Tile ceiling, installing, 90
Tile flooring, 12
estimating, 77
installing, 78–79
Triangle, 3-4-5, use of, 78–79
Trim, 13, 94
Trusses, roof, 15
Value of house, conversions and, 8
Vents and venting, 21, 63
Vinyl flooring
sheet, 82–83
tile, 78–79

W–Z
Wallboard. See Drywall
Wallcoverings, 12–13
paneling, wood, 88–89
Walls, 14, 17, 36–39
attic, building, 58–59
attic, openings in, 60–61
basement, breaching, 72, 73
basement, building, 70–71
basement, sealing, 65
codes for framing, 37
dormer, 54–55, 56
finishing, 86–89
removing, 17, 36–37
rough openings in, 38, 40, 61
Winder and spiral stairs, 19, 44
Windows, 13, 22
attic, 4, 22, 60–61
basement, 5, 22, 72, 73, 75
codes for, 22, 42
egress, 7
installing, 43
removing, 42
rough openings, 38, 40, 61
trim, 13, 94
Windowsills, basement, lowering, 72
Window wells
digging, 72–73
drains, 23
large-scale, 22, 73, 74–75
liner, installing, 74
Wires
cable, 47
copper, sizes and uses of, 46
Wiring, electrical, 15, 20, 46–47

METRIC CONVERSIONS

U.S. Units to Metric Equivalents			Metric Units to U.S. Equivalents		
To Convert From	Multiply By	To Get	To Convert From	Multiply By	To Get
Inches	25.4	Millimeters	Millimeters	0.0394	Inches
Inches	2.54	Centimeters	Centimeters	0.3937	Inches
Feet	30.48	Centimeters	Centimeters	0.0328	Feet
Feet	0.3048	Meters	Meters	3.2808	Feet
Yards	0.9144	Meters	Meters	1.0936	Yards
Square inches	6.4516	Square centimeters	Square centimeters	0.1550	Square inches
Square feet	0.0929	Square meters	Square meters	10.764	Square feet
Square yards	0.8361	Square meters	Square meters	1.1960	Square yards
Acres	0.4047	Hectares	Hectares	2.4711	Acres
Cubic inches	16.387	Cubic centimeters	Cubic centimeters	0.0610	Cubic inches
Cubic feet	0.0283	Cubic meters	Cubic meters	35.315	Cubic feet
Cubic feet	28.316	Liters	Liters	0.0353	Cubic feet
Cubic yards	0.7646	Cubic meters	Cubic meters	1.308	Cubic yards
Cubic yards	764.55	Liters	Liters	0.0013	Cubic yards

To convert from degrees Fahrenheit (F) to degrees Celsius (C), first subtract 32, then multiply by $\frac{5}{9}$.

To convert from degrees Celsius to degrees Fahrenheit, multiply by $\frac{9}{5}$, then add 32.